Doing Business in Chile and Peru

"This book is a rare comprehensive and academic book covering the social, economic, cultural, and commercial characteristics in Peru and Chile. It can be used as a standard textbook in business schools, or as a reference book for business professionals entering the Central and South American market."

—Zhixin Kang, *Professor, University of North Carolina at Pembroke, USA*

"This is a very interesting book for businesses and scholars alike. It discusses business environment and opportunities in Chile and Peru and the role of entrepreneurship and innovation in the development of businesses. In addition, it provides from a unique perspective of theory and practice the impact of the economic, politics, and social environment on trade and businesses."

—Victor Bahhouth, *Professor, University of North Carolina at Pembroke, USA*

"Drs. Spillan's and Rahman's *Doing Business in Chile and Peru—Challenges and Opportunities* offers an insightful analysis into the complexities of the current business environments of these two Latin American countries. Integrating the economic, social, historical, and political influences, the book provides researchers, scholars, and policymakers with a comprehensive view of those factors driving change and growth in Latin America. The book paints a story of the critical importance of international trade, innovation, and entrepreneurship to the future of Latin America."

—Michael Barry O'Brien, *Dean, School of Business, University of North Carolina at Pembroke, USA*

John E. Spillan · Mohammad Nakibur Rahman

Doing Business in Chile and Peru

Challenges and Opportunities

palgrave
macmillan

John E. Spillan
University of North Carolina
at Pembroke
Pembroke, NC, USA

Mohammad Nakibur Rahman
University of North Carolina
at Pembroke
Pembroke, NC, USA

ISBN 978-3-030-25072-0 ISBN 978-3-030-25073-7 (eBook)
https://doi.org/10.1007/978-3-030-25073-7

This Palgrave Macmillan imprint is published by the registered company Springer Nature Switzerland AG
The registered company address is: Gewerbestrasse 11, 6330 Cham, Switzerland

Contents

List of Figures

List of Tables

CHAPTER 1

Visiting the Profiles of Chile and Peru

1.1 Introduction

Over the last decade, South America has experienced both good and bad political economies among its members. A couple of bad examples relate to the Odebrecht construction company scandal. Grupo Odebrecht is the region's largest construction conglomerate. Its business includes major projects throughout Latin America. This company is heavily involved in the Operacao Lava Jato, or Brazil's major corruption probe associated with the huge oil company named Petrobras. Odebrecht paid lots of bribes to politicians in order to get big contracts with Petrobras (Gallas 2019). This corrupt activity has created significant turbulence among Brazilian politicians causing economic stagnation and has spread to other countries causing resignations, causing economic stagnation, and has spread to other countries such as Peru. Peru has had its own turbulence. Its former President Pedro Pablo Kuczynski was caught in a bribery scheme which caused him to resign. This was is in the midst of the efforts among the Peruvian progressives who want to make improvements and quality of life for its people better. Even in the midst of these unpopular issues occurring, the Peruvian people and business operators have been able to successfully achieve many of their economic goals.

The political and economic situation in Venezuela has become a colossal problem that has imposed huge suffering on millions of Venezuelans forcing them to migrate to bordering countries and outrightly leave for a better life outside of Venezuela. Even, Argentina, a country thought

J. E. Spillan and M. N. Rahman, *Doing Business in Chile and Peru*,
https://doi.org/10.1007/978-3-030-25073-7_1

to be economically strong and progressive has become a victim of bad public financial policy causing it to request a 57-billion-dollar loan from the International Monetary Fund (IMF). President Macri, the President of Argentina, has been unable to make progress on reviving the economy (Gillespie and Doll 2018). Even with all of this turmoil, Chile and Peru have become stars among the continent's 12 countries. Over the last decade and a half, both Chile and Peru have outclassed all of their peers in economic development. Because of their free market-oriented policies, both countries have been outperforming expectations. This has attracted good, solid foreign direct investment (FDI) from around the world, and ultimately has improved the quality of life for many of its citizens (www.bbc.com, Odebrecht Case, 2017).

1.2 Background

Throughout the world there are regions that have strong and weak economies. Many have an array of business conditions and are of interest to many investors. Latin America is unique in that the potential business opportunities are significant. While Latin America has had its economic ups and downs, some countries in this region have continually had their economic policies in the right direction. Chile and Peru are two of the stars in Latin America. They have shown that with stable politics and well thought out economic policies, economic growth and development can become a reality. Over the last two decades, both Chile and Peru have demonstrated the capability to achieve economic success and attract investment in both inward and outward FDI. Both Chile and Peru are good investment opportunities and provide both the infrastructure and the business management talent to make the investment work successfully.

One way to understand Chile and Peru is to examine their geography. The next section will provide a map and a summary of each country's highlights.

1.3 Where are Chile and Peru

1.3.1 Chile

Chile is a slim, long shaped country located along the Pacific Ocean in the southwestern part of South America (Fig. 1.1). As the map presents, Chile extends into the Punta Arena region at the Tierra del Fuego area near the South Atlantic Ocean. Because of its deep southern position on

Fig. 1.1 Map of Chile (*Source* CIA—The World Factbook [2018])

Fig. 1.2 Map of Peru (*Source* CIA—The World Factbook [2018])

the globe, it has seasons just the opposite of those in North America or many other parts of Latin America. The northern part of Chile is covered with the Atacama area or desert while the south is suitable for agriculture and vineyards which produce large amounts of wine for export. Because Chile has such a long Pacific Ocean coastline it is resourceful in seaport availability and marine life business opportunities. The seaports provide huge logistic advantages for both import and export activities.

1.3.2 Peru

Peru has a similar coastline as does Chile (Fig. 1.2). It appears that Peru's geographic dimensions are much broader and larger than that of Chile. Peru is one of the largest countries in South America. It is noted for its famous Macchu Picchu ruins located in the highlands of the Andes. Its climate varies from the very cool Andes mountains' weather to the hot Amazon Jungle region of Tingo Maria and Aucayacu. In the central coastal region or Lima, the big city area, there is a combination of cool and warm weather depending on the time of the year one is traveling in Peru. As does Chile, Peru has a very active and resourceful coastline that allows for busy seaports along the coast. While business activity is full of life all over the country, the coastline provides seaports that facilitate the easy movement of imports and exports or trade for Peruvian businesses.

1.4 The Organization of the Book

This book contains nine chapters, which comprehensively introduce and discuss the contemporary issues and ideas that are germane to the conduct of Doing Business in Latin America in the twenty-first century. The book is designed to be accessible and practical, with an emphasis on useful and applicable information. To this end, each topic is introduced with an overview, which helps to give the reader a sense of direction for what is in the chapter. Separate cases are introduced at the end of each chapter to illustrate the concepts presented in the chapter. The following outline of each chapter will show the reader what to expect and how each chapter is linked to the main theme of Doing Business in Latin America.

Chapter 1—Introduction—This chapter introduces Chile and Peru as important countries that offer major opportunities for business development. Close to 50 million people live in this area of the world, and account for a large segment of purchasing, economic, and political power in Latin America (Index Mundi 2018). Both countries have geographical attributes that allow them easy access to supply chain routes (i.e. long coastlines) and large undeveloped areas that can be converted to very productive areas with the proper investment of resources.

Chapter 2—Current Business Environment—This chapter sets forth the current business situations and trends in Chile and Peru. Presently, both of these countries continue to offer factors of production that are generally easily obtainable. Economic growth continues and is fostered by entrepreneurs who are interested in taking advantage of the attractive business environment that exist in these countries. Chile has been the economic showcase of Latin America for over two decades. Recently Peru has demonstrated great business investment opportunities.

Chapter 3—Historical Perspective on Doing Business in Chile and Peru—This chapter on the history of doing business in Chile and Peru is meant to ground the reader on various events that have helped shape Chile and Peru in general and ultimately how they do business. The chapter outlines and discusses the infrastructure of both countries and how this factor affects the conduct of business.

Chapter 4—Cultural Issues Affecting Business Activity Chile and Peru—This chapter presents a discussion of how the diversity and sameness of cultures have an impact on the economic, political, and social activities in both countries. Because of the ethnic diversity in this region, prospective business investors must take into consideration how the culture of each country can affect the conduct of business. It is a critical variable that business people and investors need to be fully aware of.

Chapter 5—Economic Climate touches upon long-term economic condition prevailing in the economy and its predictable patterns of growth, decline, potential, and movement. The term explains how generally countries economic condition varies widely. This chapter sheds more light on the economic climate of Chile and Peru particularly monetary, fiscal, and commercial systems.

Chapter 6—Latin America has been changing rapidly and is connected to the international community even more. Despite favorable macroeconomic conditions, doing business in Chile and Peru has always been a challenge due to unique negotiation pattern. This chapter sheds more light on investment in new ventures particularly business start-up financing alternatives, exchange rates, projecting cash flows, risk analysis, and financing alternatives. This chapter also discusses supply chain management issue, physical infrastructure, and issues related to sweatshops, bribery, and child labor.

Chapter 7—Establishing Businesses in Chile and Peru—This chapter discusses the main paths for establishing a business in Chile or Peru. It outlines the market challenges in each country's markets, their logistical infrastructure and how that variable has an impact on establishing a business, how negotiations are conducted in this region, and what are the perceived corporate responsibilities among companies doing business in these countries. Finally, there is a discussion of how corruption in these countries affect the establishment of business in Chile and Peru.

Chapter 8—The Marketing Process—This chapter describes and discusses the major marketing topics that relate to assessing consumer behavior and developing marketing plans to meet the needs of the customers in Chile and Peru.

Chapter 9—Chile and Peru continues to benefit from the sustained growth in globalization. There are so many unexplored economic opportunities out there. But, at the end of the day, it boils down to good governance, distribution of wealth, and trickle-down economy. While both countries pose unique challenges, the future is very bright for potential investors if the cards are properly played.

1.5 History of Business in Chile and Peru

Chile and Peru are two of the best countries to invest in Latin America. Several of the Latin American countries have been improving, however Chile and Peru are two countries that stand out. Both Chile and Peru have solid economic growth and are attracting investment interest from countries around the world (Martinez 2018). Both these countries are leaders in the extractive industries. In this context, Chile has the best economy but Peru is a very close second with one of the highest GDP growth in Latin America. The mineral resources in Peru appeal to many Canadian and American investors. While there is an existing risk of investment these countries have an above market return possibility (Martinez 2018). Many think that the United States is Peru's major trading partner however, that is not the case. China is Peru's major source for raw materials.

Chile is a success story that has not received much publicity. It has been attracting investment for decades back to the 1970s. Chile has signed agreements with Canada, Mexico, China, Japan, and the European Union. All have contributed to Chile's robust economy and economic stability (McFarlane 2018).

Chile and Peru are two of the southernmost countries in Latin America. Both share the long Pacific coastline which is a lifeline to the outside world. They share a border with each other. Historically, they have had a bittersweet relationship. In 1882, Peru and Chile signed a peace treaty but its borders were not drawn until 1929. Since that time Chile and Peru have had an up and down affiliation (Long 2014).

For a long six years a major dispute had been occurring between the two countries. The International Court of Justice in the Hague was charged deciding the fate of the maritime border that exists at the southern border of Peru and the northern border of Chile. The court ruled in favor of both nations ending a long and bitter struggle for both countries. Chile had to give up a part of the Pacific ocean to Peru yet still keep a large productive fishing area near its coastline. Both countries can celebrate and appreciate an equitable solution was found (Long 2014).

While there has been a variety of disagreements between the two countries, recent interactions have shown that they can work together on important projects that will benefit both countries. Specifically, the establishment of the Pacific Alliance trade bloc with Colombia and Mexico is an example of how both countries can work together with other countries for the benefit of the entire continent (Long 2014). Additionally, a Free Trade agreement established in 2009 has been successful and is growing.

Chile invests a great deal in Peru. In fact, Peru is the 4th largest recipient of Chilean investment in the world. There are approximately 90,000 people in Peru that are working for Chilean companies. On the other side of the border in Chile, one finds that the Peruvian population in Chile has grown to approximately 150,000 people (Long 2014).

In Chile, realistic economic development is often cluttered with pitfalls and treacherous conditions that seem to present complex barriers each step of the way. The Chilean strategy for reforms succeeded because the leaders enabled individuals to make their own choices regarding matters of vital importance. The initiatives toward privatization, innovation, and entrepreneurship energized the Chilean society. Citizens were empowered with new ideas and options to develop their entrepreneurial capabilities. This approach gave the people and the policymakers the freedom to think innovatively and promote individual growth. Along the way there have been some major challenges, but Chile continues to push forward with a positive and optimistic belief in its future.

Where are the best places for international investors to place their money? Many advisors would say a place where the investment is safe and will grow. The ever-changing global environment presents a variety of opportunities and obstacles that international managers encounter every day in their business life.

Peru alternated between military rule and democracy in the last third of the twentieth century. A violent multidecade guerilla insurgency was finally vanquished in 1990s by the government of Alberto Fujimori an authoritarian who nevertheless implemented a liberal economic reform agenda.

Pedro Pablo Kuczynski, a center-right former World Bank economist, narrowly defeated a populist campaign by Fujimori's daughter in the presidential election of 2016.

Significant foreign investment in mining and manufacturing and mining has reduced the poverty rates. Peru has entered into numerous free trade agreements with the United States and other countries and is a founding member of the Pacific Alliance (Economic Freedom 2018).

The current government is continuing its predecessor's prudent business-friendly policy framework and plans additional structural reforms that sustain Peru's economic competitiveness.

Formalizing the labor market, simplifying administrative procedures, and investing in infrastructure. Taxes for small businesses have been cut and regulations have been changed to allow easier registration of companies in regional government offices. Government corruption remains a serious problem. This factor limits foreign investors' confidence in the economy.

SOEs remain active especially in the petroleum industry.

Trade is moderately important to Peru's economy. Value of imports and exports equals 45% of GDP. Non-tariff barriers impede some trade.

Overall government policies do not significantly interfere with foreign investment.

The financial sector has undergone a gradual transformation. Credit in the private sector has increased and foreign ownership in the financial sector is growing.

Peru is a country that has been through a great deal economically and politically. The past two decades have presented opportunities and many significant challenges. Peru is a country of two sectors: the coastline which is ambitious, economically growing and offers many opportunities, and the inland which includes the Andes mountains where rugged terrain exists. In this internal sector economic development has been a struggle. Transport infrastructure outside of Lima, Peru, and the coastline cities is significantly below par and is a major constraint in moving the country forward. Large investments need to be made in infrastructure development. As such, Peru is changing but not as fast as the outside world. Modernization has been a challenge even though its telecommunication and financial sector has made significant strides in moving toward the state of the art. Overall, Peru has been making incremental progress and has promise for its future development.

1.6 Why Study Chile and Peru?

Depending on whether you are an academic or a practitioner, the study of business in Chile and Peru will be a good investment for several reasons. First, it is good to know that there are two major countries in Latin America that have demonstrated the ability to grow, develop, and provide a quality of life that is attractive to a large populace. Second, both of these countries offer a business environment that is rich in both natural and human resources. Their economic progress was not due to magic but rather on smart, methodical economic policies that have been proven successful. Third, both countries have business opportunities that are timely and future-oriented. Business investors can be encouraged to explore the various paths that are available for them to pursue good business development. Finally, just studying Chile and Peru provides a different perspective on how economic development is done even when there are a variety of institutional constraints.

1.7 Who Will Benefit?

The readers of this book with benefit. They will obtain an objective perspective on doing business in Chile and Peru. They will advance their knowledge and possibly open new trends of thought about the structure and the nature of business in these now famous Latin American countries. Practitioners will receive a survey of objective scenarios that can give potential investors an understanding of the pros and cons, strengths and weaknesses of investing in these countries. For academics it just provides an alternative point of view on two stable and valuable countries in Latin America.

1.8 Is There a Future for Business Development FDI and Entrepreneurship?

Without question, there are huge opportunities for FDI development and entrepreneurship. In fact, both of these are occurring as this book is being written. In Chile, the National Council for Innovation manages the innovation system in that country and has followed many start-ups and new ventures. In Peru, the council of Technology and innovation develops policies and coordinates activities (Spillan and Ramsey 2019). Both countries have recognized the significance and importance of innovation and entrepreneurship as these items relate to the future of business development.

1.9 Discussion

Chile and Peru are important countries in Latin America. They have a high ranking in almost all reliable "International Doing Business Charts". While Chile has a continuing reputation of being the more successful country economically and politically, Peru has made major progress since the beginning of the twenty-first century. Investors who are interested in forward-thinking economies, Chile and Peru are examples of economies which have implemented public policies that are pro-business and pro-free market. These policies have strengthened their physical, economic, and political infrastructures and have enhanced the quality of life in each of these countries. It must be understood that of the two, Chile, since the early 1990s, has manifested incredible stability and has been the showcase of business development for Latin America. Chile has advanced in various levels of business development but one area that sticks out is that of entrepreneurship and innovation. Significant progress has been made in Chile regarding both the infrastructure for entrepreneurship, i.e. education and the implementation of entrepreneurship and innovation. The value added to the Chilean economy from entrepreneurship and innovation has been substantial when compared to the other Latin American economies.

Even though Peru has not had all of the success that Chile has encountered, Peru has become a member of the prestigious Pacific Alliance trading bloc. This membership has given Peru a huge bump forward and an opportunity to expand its trade horizons among its own peer countries in Latin America.

As previously stated, Peru and Chile are very important economies and demonstrate how good public policies can move a country toward prosperity and better the quality of life among its citizens.

1.10 Conclusion

Business people and investors are always interested in finding and exploring new business development opportunities whether it be from actual enterprise construction with a brick and mortar structure, export or import activities, or a virtual office where independent contractors can provide a venue, distribution, or service center. Chile and Peru are considered two of the best countries in Latin America for doing business. Their stable and growing economies which have demonstrated great market potential is very encouraging and worthy of serious consideration. The fast pace of the global economy presents many uncertainties for the business persons. No one knows what the future holds for business opportunities in Chile or Peru. However, based on past experiences, historical business, and economic data, the business development future in these two countries seems bright.

References

Chile Map CIA—The World Factbook. 2018. https://www.cia.gov/library/publications/the-world-factbook/geos/ci.html.

Economic Freedom. 2018. Index of Economic Freedom, https://www.heritage.org/index/country/peru. Accessed October 20, 2018.

Gallas, Daniel. 2019. Brazil's Odebrecht Corruption Scandal Explained, BBC News, South America, https://www.bbc.com/news/business-39194395. Accessed April 27, 2019.

Gillespie, Patrick, and Ignacio Olivera Doll. 2018. Argentina Gets $57 Billion as IMF Doubles Down on Record Bailout, https://www.bloomberg.com/news/articles/2018-09-26/argentina-gets-57-billion-as-imf-doubles-down-on-record-bailout. Accessed April 27, 2019.

Index Mundi. 2018. https://www.indexmundi.com/factbook/compare/peru.chile/demographics.

Long, Gideon. 2014. Chile-Peru: Moving on from the Past, BBC News, Santiago, https://www.bbc.com/news/world-latin-america-25924381. Accessed November 26, 2018.

Martinez, Ricardo Henao. 2018. The 3 Best Latin American Countries to Invest In, ETF Analysis, Seeking Alpha, https://seekingalpha.com/article/4212379-3-best-latin-american-countries-invest. Accessed November 26, 2018.

McFarlane, Greg. 2018. Top 4 Places to Invest in Latin America, Investopedia, https://www.investopedia.com/articles/investing/111214/best-4-places-invest-latin-america.asp. Accessed November 26, 2018.

Odebrecht Case: Politicians Worldwide Suspected in Bribery Scandal, December 15, 2017, https://www.bbc.com/news/world-latin-america-41109132. Accessed September 21, 2018.

Odebrecht Case: Politicians Worldwide Suspected in Bribery Scandal, December 15, 2017, https://www.bbc.com/news/world-latin-america-41109132. Accessed September 24, 2018.

Peru Map CIA—The World Factbook. 2018. https://www.cia.gov/library/publications/the-world-factbook/geos/pe.html.

Spillan, John, and Jase Ramsey. 2019. *Navigating Commerce in Latin America: Options and Obstacles*. New York and London: Routledge and Taylor & Francis.

CHAPTER 2

Business Trends in Chile and Peru

2.1 Introduction

Globalization refers to the trend toward greater economic, cultural, political, and technological interdependence between and among countries, institutions, and economies (Wild and Wild 2019).

Globalization also refers to the convergence in buyer preferences in markets worldwide. Global products and global competition epitomize many markets and industries. Globalization has been integrated into all businesses such as technology, accounting, automobiles, and consumer goods and many more (Wild and Wild 2019).

The impacts of globalization have been as follows:

a. Reducing marketing costs
b. Creating new market opportunities and equalizing uneven income streams
c. Addressing local buyer needs
d. Beginning to address global sustainability (Wild and Wild 2019).

2.2 Background

Over and over again the literature and popular press indicate that Chile is the showcase of economic and developmental success in Latin America. Since the 1990s Chile has been growing, changing, and developing.

J. E. Spillan and M. N. Rahman, *Doing Business in Chile and Peru*,
https://doi.org/10.1007/978-3-030-25073-7_2

Good policymaking, and political stability have been two of the hallmark factors that have propelled Chile to its extraordinary level of economic success. It has given Chileans a better quality of life and more hope for the future of their country. Chile has strong economic fundamentals that have continued to produce excellent growth. In fact, the growth in the first half of 2018 has been the strongest since 2012. The economic outlook is encouraging yet cautious because lots of threats exist in the world economy. That is why Chile has strived to implement good economic policies to lessen the risk and impact of any downturn (Chile: Concluding Statement 2018).

Peru has surprised many watchers of economic development in Latin America. For a time in the 1990s, many thought that Peru would never come together and rid itself of the instability and turbulence that was so pervasive in the country. Today in 2019 we can see Peru as an economically growing country with lots of hope for future development. Yes, Peru has some weak areas especially in the altiplano and some of the southeastern areas, but plans are focusing on making those areas prosperous too. Peru, presently, has set the foundation for positive economic growth with some good public policies, stable government, and an eagerness to move forward and implement its progressive plans. Peru's economic performance has been very good with inflation low, its fiscal position stronger. However, the continuation of the 2014 Odebrecht corruption scandal has contributed to a slowdown in GDP Growth in 2017 (Peru: Concluding Statement 2018).

2.3 Business Environment

The business environments in both countries, Chile and Peru, have been very good for foreign direct investment (FDI) and for domestic investment. On the international stage, both countries have received respectable scores on the Global Competitiveness Index Report. This index evaluates the countries on twelve pillars. This report measures each country on a set of institutions, policies, and factors that are considered the factors that drive sustainable current and medium-term economic prosperity (Schwab 2018). The twelve pillars used to measure global competitiveness are as follows: institutions, infrastructure, macroeconomic environment, health and primary education, higher education and training, goods market efficiency, labor market efficiency, financial market development, technological readiness, market size, business sophistication, and innovation. Rising competitiveness means rising prosperity (Schwab 2018). For the 2018 Global Competitiveness Report, Chile scored 33 out of 140 countries measured

Table 2.1 Chile's economic indicators

Economic indicators	*2015*	*2016*	*2017*
Real GDP % change	2.1	1.6	2.1
Consumer price %	4.4	2.7	3.0
Merchandise trade (billions of dollars)			
Exports	62.2	59.1	62.5
Imports	58.7	55.8	59.0
Current account balance as % of GDP	−2.1	−1.7	−1.6

Source Gendreau et al. (2018)

while Peru scored 70 out of 140 countries measured. International competitiveness is a measure of the relative cost of goods/services from a country. Countries which can produce the same quality of goods at a lower cost are said to be more competitive (Schwab 2018).

With these elements of competitiveness in mind, we now turn to what has been going on in Chile and Peru.

2.3.1 *Chile*

With the election of Sabastian Pinera, the economic conditions that presently exist in Chile appear to be stable. There is at present no intention of repealing previous President Michele Bachelet's policies regarding corporate tax, education, and labor market requirements. According to the World Economic Forum, Chile's ease of doing business report fell from a high ranking of 34 to 57 during the Bachelet administration. However, this ranking was eliminated because the methodologists involved in the statistical analysis indicated that there was a methodical error and the ranking is being reversed now. Most accounts indicate that Chile is one of the most business-friendly countries in Latin America.

Table 2.1 summarizes Chile's year to year macroeconomic performance for a recent three-year period. It appears that Chile has sustained a relatively stable growth pattern during this period of time.

2.3.2 *Peru*

Peru fell 4 places in the World Bank's 2018 ease of doing business ranking from 58 out of 190 countries measured. One of Peru's major goals is to

Table 2.2 Peru's economic indicators

Economic indicators	*2016*	*2017*[e]	*2018*[f]
Real GDP % change	3.9	2.6	3.7
Consumer price %	3.2	1.4	2.3
Merchandise trade (billions of dollars)			
Exports	37.0	42.5	45.0
Imports	35.1	38.2	41.0
Current account balance as % of GDP	−4.8	−2.7	0.0

Source Gendreau et al. (2018)
[e]estimated
[f]forecasted

Table 2.3 Capital inflows to Peru and Chile is outlined in the subsequent table

In billions of dollars ($)	*2016*	*2017*[e]	*2018*[f]
Chile	5.9	2.4	4.4
Peru	7.0	8.2	8.2

Source Gendreau et al. (2018)
[e]estimated
[f]forecasted

bring more workers into the formal economy. One incentive is for Peru's government to create a new tax bracket for small business and make it easier to obtain business licenses and company/business registration. In addition, there is a need, desire, and will to promote public/private partnerships in order to attract investment in Peru's infrastructure.

Table 2.2 summarizes Peru' s year to year macroeconomic performance for a recent three-year period. It appears that Peru has sustained a relatively stable and very good growth pattern during this period of time.

The Odebrecht scandal in Peru distributed $29 million dollars to various politicians between 2005 and 2014. Former Presidents Toledo, Garcia, Humala, and Kuczynski have all be implicated in receiving illegal payments from the Odebrecht Construction Company.

The foregoing tables provide important information about Chile and Peru's business environment. In Table 2.3 we see that cash inflows for Chile have been steady and for Peru more than double than that of Chile.

In Table 2.4 we see that the ease of doing business rankings for both countries are generally in the same category. So, investors interested in either country can see that they are about the same in ranking for ease of doing business.

Table 2.4 World Bank ease of doing business rankings

Country	*2018 rank*	*2017 rank*
Chile	*	57
Peru	58	54

*As mentioned in text—methodological error in survey
Source Gendreau et al. (2018)

Table 2.5 Global Innovation Rankings—out of 120 economies

Country	*2017 rank*	*2016 rank*
Chile	46	44
Peru	70	71

Source Gendreau et al. (2018), according to Global Innovation Index

Finally, Table 2.5 shows that Chile is way ahead of Peru in terms of innovation. Start-Up Chile has been the driving force pushing Chile to the forefront of innovation. This initiative has received worldwide recognition and made major progress in innovative ideas among Chilean entrepreneurs.

Latin America as a whole tends to lag other regions on innovation, however Chile has become the leader in this area with its Start-Up initiative.

2.4 Description of Popular Business Ventures

Peru's agricultural sector is very strong. It produces approximately 240,000 metric tons of wheat annually. The wheat is used in processed foods.

Peru's textile industry has major competition from Vietnam enterprises. Exports for 2018 were approximately $1.8 billion dollars.

2.4.1 Overview

Peru's government has continued to implement fiscal and monetary policies. The government is an appropriate business friend and supportive of business development and trade (www.export.gov, 2018). One of the major tests facing Peru is corruption. With the occurrence of the fallout from the Odebrecht scandal, Peru has been confronted with some uncertainty. Peru is striving for entry into the Organization for Economic Cooperation and Development (OECD) membership by 2021 so Peru needs to make sure that all of the economic, political, and legal matters are in order before becoming a member of this prestigious group. The OECD is an organization that works to promote economic growth, prosperity, and sustainable development.

Another area of concern relates to the damage that was hurled at Peru due to the 2017 el Niño storms. The storm caused $3.1 billion dollars of loss in damages to various infrastructure, houses, agricultural products, etc. (www.export.gov, 2018).

2.5 How Is Globalization Affecting Market Structures and Business Opportunities?

Trading Blocs—i.e. European Union, Pacific Alliance, etc. effect on business and marketing.

Major trends in business activity in Chile and Peru.

Chile is a country that has grown to become the "Showcase of Latin America". After significant political and economic turmoil in the 1970s through 1988 with Salvador Allende and Augusto Pinochet's military dictatorships, Chile went through significant turbulence, pain, and uncertainty because of the political and economic policies of these two regimes. With the election of Presidents Patricio Aylwin in the early 1990s and later (1994–1995) Eduardo Frei, the military influence was reduced and confidence in the country's institutions was restored.

Ricardo Lagos Escobar, a Social Democrat won the 1999–2000 presidential election and served until 2006. He was a major opponent of General Pinochet. Removing Gen Pinochet allowed Chile to change its path to tranquility and progress. Normalcy began to return to Chile during the Lagos presidency. He turned the economy around, fixed the infrastructure and transportation system, and became a well-respected president.

From 2006 to the present 2018, Chile has had ups and down to the economy but overall it has moved in the right direction. Consistent and effective macroeconomic policy over the last two decades has helped Chile become a stellar performer in the Latin American environment. In fact, Chile is among the most economically attractive country in Latin America. Increased trade, great political stability, and good policies have made Chile a great place to do business. This business attractiveness has evolved because of the election of politicians who have promoted positive policies for business development. In recent times, the opportunities have grown more appealing. The recent chronology of Chile's political administration tells a great deal about why the country has continued to be stable and prosperous.

In 2006 Michelle Bachelet became president. Her term was steady and stable. She promoted a free market philosophy which continued the growth and development of Chile.

In 2010 Sabastian Pinera was elected president. His administration continued solid and effective political and economic policies.

In 2013 Michelle Bachelet again was elected and returned to the effective policies that have made Chile an attractive business investment.

In 2017 Sabastian Pinera won the election and took office in March of 2018. Based on the last year's observations President Pinera has been a major advocate for free-market approach to economic development. His administration has been a leader in pushing innovation and entrepreneurship both internally and externally. So, one could say that the consistency in policies and free market approach have contributed heavily to Chile's political and economic stability.

Chile's business revolves around its industrial and service sectors. These two sectors contribute to about 96% of the GDP. Copper mining and its export to markets around the world along with the manufactured products such as agro-food, chemicals, and wood are important business arenas that have brought economic growth and prosperity to Chile. Additionally, fishing, viticulture, and fruit are popular areas of business operations. Broken down according to business sectors are as follows:

Agricultural sector represents 4.3% of GDP and Employment in this sector is about 10%

Industrial sector represents 32% of GDP and its Employment in this sector is about 23%

Service sector contributes 64.4% of GDP and its Employment in this sector is about 67% (Chile: Economic and Political 2018).

2.6 The Current Doing Business Framework in Chile and Peru

2.6.1 *Chile*

Ninety percent of goods entering and leaving Chile use maritime routes. Ports are critical to Chile's business success. With 6000 km of coastline, it has 56 terminals and ports. Of that 56, ten of them are public and 14 are private ports or terminals. Thirty-two of them are exclusively private.

In addition, there are fifteen mining and seventeen oil ports (Embassy of Kingdom 2018).

FDI is an important area of Chilean business development. This has been sustained due to overseas investment. This business approach has helped in technological development with specialized know-how and contributions to the acquisition of resources and tech development (Global Reach 2018).

2.6.2 *Business Culture*

Chileans are well connected with the world and open to change, yet not willing to surrender their values. 95.5% of Chileans speak Spanish and 10.2% speak English. Most native English speakers who are in Chile need translators.

Religion is important and plays an important role in the social and political life of Chileans.

Family is the center of Chilean life. Family businesses are popular, and many small businesses are of this type. Family businesses manifest a positive appearance in Chile.

Business culture in Chile is different than in other Latin American countries. Value of time is a key issue. Chile is surprisingly the most punctual country in Latin America.

2.6.3 *Peru*

Coups have repeatedly interrupted civil constitutional government in Peru. In the most recent period of military rule (1968–1980) General Juan Velasco Alvarado overthrew Pres. Fernando Belaunde Terry. Elections in 1990 ushered in a decade that saw a dramatic turnaround in the economy with President Fujimori's election. There was a significant reduction in the guerrilla activity however the use of authoritarian measures had a negative impact on the economy and caused Mr. Fujimori to be removed. There was much uncertainty, fear, and diminished growth and development (Country Review—Peru 2018) (Table 2.6).

Peru enacted anti-corruption laws in October 2016 as scandals plagued several Peruvian politicians.

Table 2.6 Political Risk Index

PoliticalRisk Index—measured on a 0–10 scale with 10 indicating the riskiest
Chile—9, Peru—7
Political Stability Index—measure is the same as 0–10 above
Chile—9, Peru—7.5

2.6.4 *Chile*

Chile leads most of the Latin American countries in competitiveness, income per capita, and economic freedom. It has low corruption and is the most stable and prosperous country in the Latin American environment. Chile is the largest producer of copper in the world.

Peru has many of the first world amenities and ancient world touristic adventures with Machu Picchu being one of the 7 wonders of the world. It has become one of the most visited phenomena in the Western Hemisphere. In addition, Peru has the Amazon rain forest with the archeological sites either on the way to the sites or surrounding them (www.infoplease, 2018).

2.6.5 *Peru*

Potatoes are an important product in Peru. They are economically and socially important to most of the population. About 1 million families cultivate potatoes resulting in almost 4 million tons of potatoes. In the highland area of Peru, such as Cuzco, potatoes are the main crop farmers harvest. This crop becomes the main source of food and cash income. Additionally, harvesting potatoes provides jobs for a great many people who live in the highlands. Besides the economic value, the highlanders receive cultural benefits by following the ancestral customs with the potato harvest.

Over the years the production and consumption of potatoes has declined. To address the decrease in potato consumption an NGO named Potato Innovation and Competitiveness in Peru or INCOPA has taken on the role of improving the potato production. The NGO has been promoting innovations in natural potato production and marketing. Using applied research and development (R&D) methods called participatory chain was developed to capitalize on the biodiversity that is associated with potatoes, their culinary, nutrition, and cultural attributes. This approach to innovation includes participation of the private and public sectors to advance innovation that can make potatoes and other crops competitive in the domestic and world markets (Ordinola et al. 2014).

The tourism industry in Peru is a hot industry. Analysis of growth trends and progress for 2015–2020.

Peru is committed to free trade and has positioned itself to be a regional transport location. Foreign investment in Peru is ruled by the 1991 Promotion of Foreign Investment Law and Framework Law on Growth and Private Investment which establishes equal treatment of national and foreign capital. Foreign capital can be invested in all sectors of economic activity without prior authorization (Modor Intelligence 2017). There are a variety of challenges such as corruption, bureaucracy, conflict with native people over natural resources, language barrier, and technology. Peru's policies allow foreign-owned companies to set up corp, closed corp, LLCs, Joint ventures, distributors, or PC type business.

Peru is the main trading partner with Chile. Exports in textiles, chemicals, and pharmaceuticals account for 59.4% of Peru's GDP (Sherlock Communications 2018).

2.6.5.1 *Peruvian Textile Markets*

Young weavers in Cuzco area, in the highland of Andes. The young weavers learn the ancient technique from members of the family. The ideas and tradition are given from one generation to another. The weaving process demonstrates the productivity of the Peruvian culture. The traditional values are expressed in the weaving work produced by the indigenous weavers. The Artisanal markets offer a variety of traditional textile products produced by indigenous people who are descendants of the ancient Inca empire. These textiles are handmade and can take weeks or in some cases months to make. Industrial production of the same type products and artisanal are produced more rapidly and in larger quantities at a lower price. This has created real competition for the traditional artisans who now have to struggle with the new competition. One method that these Artisans are using is a process of selling to a third party who pays them less than 50% of final retail price. This is really the only way Artisans can compete.

Artisans need assistance in business know-how and marketing. They need advice on how to grow and sustain their businesses. Opportunities exist and can produce great Artisan products. Some way an interface between the Artisans and business consultants need to begin (Martinez 2017).

Table 2.7 Internet users penetration—Chile and Peru—2013–2019 internet users (in millions)

Country	*2013*	*2014*	*2015*	*2016*	*2017*	*2018*	*2019*
Chile	10.7	11.6	12.3	12.7	12.9	13.2	13.4
Peru	13.0	14.5	16.0	17.6	19.0	20.1	21.3
Internet growth %							
Peru	14.7	11.7	10.4	9.6	8.0	6.2	5.6
Chile	8.5	7.8	6.6	2.5	2.2	1.9	1.7
Internet user penetration % of population							
Chile	62.4	66.7	70.5	71.7	72.7	73.5	74.2
Peru	43.5	48.1	52.6	57.1	51.1	64.3	67.3

Source Peru's Consumers and Advertisers (2015)

Peru has three different segments or natural regions: the coast, the sierras, and the selva. Each of these segments are unique in attributes that impact human settlement and their economic and technological development. Because of the geography and a cautious approach to the digital media, and subscriptions among consumers. This has caused advertisers to slow their movement and budgeting toward digital advertising. They speculate that by 2019 that the expenditures for digital advertising will double reaching $153.2 million.

Some statistics can provide a more enlightened perspective (Table 2.7).

The foregoing tables provide a snapshot of the trends in Internet penetration in both Chile and Peru. Clearly, both countries have significant Internet availability among their populations.

Peruvian consumer behavior has developed substantially over the past decades. This is especially true with regard to the use of the Internet with people sharing their preferences for certain brands and product types.

Peruvians are rational consumers and as a result quality is the main factor when they make purchase decisions. Durable goods are purchases primarily form brand name products. Everyday products are usually purchased based on price and availability. Peruvians ambitiously seek out promotions and discounts which explain why e-commerce is growing at such a rapid pace. Leisure time and activities are also popular (Country Profile 2016).

Culture affects the relationship between innovation and growth. Innovation needs to be aligned to culture, economics, and institutional context to produce positive outcomes. Innovation is at the core of entrepreneurship. Innovation provides new products, processes, methods, new markets, new supply methods, and new organizations. Additionally, it increases the learning that ultimately affects competitive advantage. As it increases the competitive advantage hence there is growth.

Culture is a multilevel construct. National culture has an entrepreneurial subculture which develops an organizational culture. This level of cultural orientation has an impact on the practices that business owners apply in their businesses. Cultural practices indicate how owners go about managing their businesses (Rauch et al. 2013).

2.6.6 Chile

Chile has been evaluated as one of the best emerging economies in Latin America. It has a stable economy, lots of transparency with reliability, and international connectedness. It has the highest per capita GDP in the region with the most competitive ranking in the region. It has a great business climate and has become a hub for international FDI. It has a vibrant entrepreneurial environment where innovation is a major theme and where its concept of Start-Up has gained worldwide recognition. This feature has gained Chile the 6th rank on the GEM index (Killer-Facts 2017).

Some of the major business opportunities that exist in Chile are listed below:

Agrobusiness—major opportunity due to the technology in fruits and food production.

Maritime—fishing is a great area for investment and R&D. Fish processing techniques always need improvement and new and improved methods to reduce pollution in the sea and fishing areas.

Mining—copper has always been at the top of the list. Presently Chile has 53 investment projects in the number of billions of dollars of investment money coming into Chile.

Retail—significant growth available in this area. E-commerce and model specialty clothing stores are growing in Chile.

Tourism—there are many attractive and important touristic destinations to explore. Chile has a huge potential in this area.

Construction—Chile has great potential as the economy continues to grow. Building manufacturing and waste management entities are highly viable opportunities for growth and development (Killer-Facts 2017).

FDI is critically important for growth and development. Fortunately, Chile has received a major increase in FDI over the past decade. This increase in FDI has contributed to its competitiveness and has provided inputs to technological development, specialized knowledge, innovation, and entrepreneurship (TMF Group 2018).

Even though there has been rapid business development in Chile, there still exist some business challenges that confront entering businesses. These challenges are presented below:

1. The World Bank has ranked Chile as 32nd in the world for ease of doing business. However, there are a variety of procedures and documents that prospective business people have to attend to. Such things as registration, articles of incorporation, tax registration, working licenses all take time and money to establish a new business.
2. Construction permits—procuring construction permits can be a lengthy process. There are 15 requirements associated with various agencies that have to be completed.
3. Electricity connection—this process can be short or lengthy depending on how prepared one is at time of application.
4. Registering a project is also a lengthy process. Registering titles and getting certificates takes time,
5. Getting credit is difficult and hence business owner should be prepared to deal with this challenge.
6. Trading across borders is easy but it may take a while to complete the 15 steps.
7. Enforcing contracts is relatively efficient however filing and serving documents takes time.
8. Culture—one of the prime requirements in Chile and for that matter in any business is establishing trust. Building rapport with people and business associates and connections is really more important than many other business issues (TMF Group 2018).

Chile ranks 56 out of 190 countries in the world for ease of doing business. It has improved some of the challenges of starting a business. A couple of those areas relate to (a) replace hard copy print filing of accounting documents with electronic filing and (b) contract enforcement allows the plaintiff to file complaints electronically, or a new e-system has been implemented (World Bank 2019).

2.7 Discussion

Almost all data indicates that besides Mexico, Chile is the strongest country economically and politically in Latin America. While it has had some ugly time during the 1960s through the 1980s the last thirty years have demonstrated nothing but continuous growth, positive development, and readiness to do business. Its policymaking has been analytical, methodical, and from all indications very successful. Chile has copied some of the business and economic techniques employed by its US and European neighbors. Using these practices, Chile has recorded excellent performance and continues to be recognized as a formidable economic power in Latin America.

Likewise, Peru has had a reliable and positive business environment over the last decade. Yes, it has had some turbulent years with the Fujimori regime and the Kaczynski scandal, but even with these crises, Peru has maintained a very solid and positive economic trajectory. Most of the economic indicator suggest that Peru not only has the potential to grow and develop more, but more robustly than in the past. Its ability to establish trade relationships with countries around the world has been a strong part of its economic strategy. Attracting foreign investment by making it easier to start and operate a business in Peru has also been a major plus in its economic development efforts. The future seems bright and the policymakers appear to have the appropriate competencies for further positive economic development.

2.8 Conclusion

Chile and Peru are neighbors, partners, competitors, and rivals. Many of the attributes that exist in Chile also are seen in Peru. One would have to conclude however, that Chile does seem to have a little bit more sophistication than Peru. Its history of economic development has been stronger, and its business policy development has given Chile a better spotlight and recognition as the place to invest in Latin America. Chile's ability to remain stable both politically and economically over a long period of time (more than 30 years) is clearly an obvious advantage.

In contrast, Peru has not had all of the physical and political positives as Chile. The cities of Lima, Trujillo, Chimbote are the main geographic engines of economic growth, while Cuzco, Puno, and Arequipa are mountainous remote cities that have large indigenous populations which have not made much economic progress over the last 100 years. While these areas are not detracting from Peru's economic development they are not contributing substantially. Because these cities are located in areas that are difficult to reach by land, and other transportation, this circumstance has a negative impact on marketing and supply chain efforts in getting goods and services to people living in these areas. As a result, business and economic development is not as ambitious or thriving as it is in Lima, Trujillo, and Chimbote. These cities have good road, sea, and air transportation. Such a situation makes it much easier for business development.

2.8.1 *Business Examples*

The following presents some successful businesses that have been established in Peru and Chile over the years have demonstrated success to its owners, employees, community, and country:

A good example of a small but successful Peruvian company is La Iberica. Juan Vidaurrazaga Menchaca a Spanish immigrant to Peru founded this company in 1909. It continues operation today in Arequipa, Peru. Using the cacao fruit found in the Andes mountains around the famous city of Cuzco, chocolate is produced in La Iberica's factory.

The company's traditional recipe and formulas produce various combinations of Chocolate product that are wanted by travelers from around the world. La Iberica's key to success is attention to detail, using century old traditions, hand and modern mechanized machinery along with the application of technology. Over the years the management of La Iberica has expanded its product lines with other forms of delicious sweets such as toffees, mazapanes, and several other confectionaries.

La Iberica has a famous reputation for excellent and high-quality products. It also has an excellent reputation among the Peruvian Industrial network, a major business association in Peru (La Iberica 2019).

2.8.2 *Kingston Family Vineyards*

Another example is the Kingston Family Vineyards. Carl John Kingston founded this company in the early 1990s while visiting Chile searching for copper and gold. Because this venture never came to fruition, while in Chile exploring C.J. discovered a large dairy and cattle ranch in Chile's Casablanca Valley. They purchased the place and settled in calling it the farm. As time passed the Kingston's developed the area and in 1998 planned the first grapevines. One approach led to another and eventually the planting became successful. Today the Kingston Vineyards have a great reputation and are known as one of the best in production of pinot wines. Currently, their wines are advertised and consumed by individuals, restaurants, and other businesses all over the world.

Starting from nothing, this family has created a business that now is productive, profitable, and in continuous operation. It has a great future in Chile. Another example of how an investor being in the right place, Chile, and using his/her ingenuity can develop a successful and sustainable company in a stable and prosperous country (Kingston Family Vineyard 2019).

References

Advertising and Marketing in Peru. 2016. https://www.nordeatrade.com/en/explore-new-market/peru/marketing. Accessed February 14, 2019.

Albuja, Julio Alejandro, and Leonardo Javiar Merino. 2017. Analysis of the Competitive Factors of Business in Chile. *Espacios* 38 (29): 11.

Chile: Concluding Statement. 2018. https://www.imf.org/en/News/Articles/2018/09/20/chile-staff-concluding-statement-of-the-2018-article-iv-mission. Accessed March 21, 2019.

Chile: Economic and Political Outline. 2018. https://en.portal.santandertrade.com/analyse-markets/chile/economic-political-outlineChil. Accessed January 26, 2019.

Chile Profile—Timeline. 2017. www.bbc.com/news/world-latinamerica-19356356.

Country Profile Chile. 2016. https://www.nordeatrade.com/en/explore-new-market/chile/marketing. Accessed February 14, 2019.

Country Profile Peru. 2016. Advertising and Marketing in Peru. https://www.nordeatrade.com/en/explore-new-market/peru/marketing. Accessed February 14, 2019.

Country Review (Peru). 2018. Country Watch. http://www.countrywatch.com/. Accessed January 27, 2019.

Devaux, André, Douglas Horton, Claudio Velasco, Graham Thiele, Gastón López, Thomas Bernet, Iván Reinoso, and Miguel Ordinola. 2009. Collective Action for Market Chain Innovation in the Andes. *Journal of Food Policy* 34: 31–38.

Embassy of Kingdom of the Netherlands in Chile Ministry of Foreign Affairs June 2018.

Gendreau, Brian C., and Timothy McLendon. 2018. *2018 Latin American Business Environment Report*. UF Center for Latin American Studies, University of Florida. https://www.sherlockcomms.com/peru-pr/market-overview/, https://www.mordorintelligence.com/industry-reports/market-entry-tourism-and-hotel-industry-in-peru. Accessed February 14, 2019.

Global Reach Local Knowledge. 2018. Top 10 Challenges of Doing Business in Chile. http://www.tmf-group.com/en/news-insights/business-culture/top-challenges-chile/.

Kingston Family Vineyard. 2019. https://www.kingstonvineyards.com/terms. Accessed April 19, 2019.

Killer-Facts-Chile. 2017. http://www.syite.com/2017/06/killer-facts-opportunities-business-chile/2017. Accessed February 21, 2019.

La Iberica. 2019. https://prezi.com/4i21bfavbxf9/la-iberica/. Accessed April 19, 2019.

Martinez, Lourdes. 2017. Insights into the Traditional Textile Market of Peru. Net Impact. https://www.netimpact.org/blog/insights-into-the-traditional-textile-market-of-peru.

Modor Intelligence. 2017. https://www.mordorintelligence.com/industry-reports/market-entry-tourism-and-hotel-industry-in-peru. Accessed February 14, 2019.

Ordinola, Miguel, and Andre Devaux. 2014. *The PMCA and Potato Market Chain Innovation in Peru*, 1–8. Papa Andina Innovation Brief 3.

Peru's Consumers and Advertisers Slowly Coming to Digital Life: Advertisers Will Spend $81.8 Million to Connect with Internet Users in Peru in 2015. November 18, 2015. https://www.emarketer.com/Article/Perursquos-Consumers-Advertisers-Slowly-Coming-Digital-Life/1013243. Accessed February 14, 2019.

Peru: Concluding Statement. 2018. https://www.imf.org/en/News/Articles/2018/05/22/ms052318-peru-staff-concluding-statement-of-the-2018-article-iv-mission. Accessed March 21, 2019.

Rauch, Andreas, Michael Frese, Zhong-Ming Wang, Jens Unger, Lozada Maria, Vita Kupcha, and Tanga Spirna. 2013. National Culture and Cultural Orientation of Owners Affecting the Innovation-Growth Relationship in 5 Countries. *Entrepreneurship and Regional Development* 25 (9–10): 732–755.

Schwab, Klaus. 2018. *The Global Competitiveness Report*. World Economic Forum. http://www3.weforum.org/docs/GCR2018/05FullReport/TheGlobalCompetitivenessReport2018.pdf. Accessed April 13, 2019.

TMF Group. http://www.tmf-group.com/en/news-insights/business-culture/top-challenges-chile/. Accessed February 21, 2019.

Wild, John J., and Kenneth L. Wild. 2019. *International Business: The Challenges of Globalization*, 9th ed. New York and London: Pearson Publishing.

World Bank. 2019. *Doing Business Report 2019: Training for Reforms*. A World Bank Flagship Report, 16th ed. http://www.worldbank.org/content/dam/doingbusiness/media/Annual-Report/English/DB2019-report.webversion.pdf.

CHAPTER 3

Historical Perspective on Doing Business in Chile and Peru

3.1 Introduction

Both Chile and Peru have interesting and similar and controversial histories. The commonness relates to much of their culture, their heritage as descendants of Spain and their language. Since Chile and Peru are geographically close they share the Pacific Ocean, their Northern and Southern border, respectively. Peru's history is dominated by the Inca Empire with its elegance, geographic expansiveness, and its great contribution to the historical archives of Latin America. Peru has an extensive population of indigenous inhabitants mostly of the Aymara group. Most of the indigenous people live in the altiplano or the Andes sections of Peru. Typical indigenous homes and living arrangements can be seen all over the Andes. Many of these inhabitants have retained many of the customs from the past.

In Chile, the Mapuche group live in the southern part of the country. Their homes are not as representative of indigenous home that Peru's indigenous people possess. It appears that the Mapuches have assimilated into the Chilean culture more than the indigenous of Peru.

Over the last three decades, Peru has had its ups and downs. Recently however since the beginning of the twenty-first century, Peru has been showing real economic and political progress. Yes, it has hit some speed bumps along the way but by and large it has made some real progress. The Fujimori administration's turbulence and the recent Kaczynski administration's failures have been examples that have caused business people to pause and think about the stability of Peruvian economy. Even with these

J. E. Spillan and M. N. Rahman, *Doing Business in Chile and Peru*,
https://doi.org/10.1007/978-3-030-25073-7_3

distractions, Peru has been chosen to be part of the prestigious Pacific Alliance, a regional integration of four of the most stable and prosperous countries in Latin America—Chile, Peru, Colombia, and Mexico. Being part of this group has signaled to the world that Peru is not only a major regional player but also a recognized world player.

3.2 Background

3.2.1 Peru

Peru is a country located in the southwestern part of South America with a coastline that extends along the Pacific Ocean. Five countries border Peru, Bolivia, Brazil, Chile Colombia, and Ecuador. With its geographic arrangement, Peru is able to have intercountry trade, business and political interaction among its five neighbors with relative ease. Peru's population is approximately 31 million citizens with three primary languages spoken among its people: Spanish 84%, Quechaua 13%, and Aymara 1.4%. The literacy rate in Peru is 94.2% indicating that a great many Peruvian citizens are literate and have the basic educational requirements to work in a variety of business environments (Peru Country Review 2018).

Peru alternated between military rule and democracy in the last third of the twentieth century. A violent multidecade guerilla insurgency was finally vanquished in the 1990s by the government of Alberto Fujimori an authoritarian who nevertheless implemented a liberal economic reform agenda. Pedro Pablo Kuczynski, a center-right former World Bank economist, narrowly defeated a populist campaign by Fujimori's daughter in the presidential election of 2016.

Significant foreign investment in mining and manufacturing and mining has reduced the poverty rates. Peru has entered into numerous free trade agreements with the United States and other countries. It also is one of the founding members of the Pacific Alliance (www.heritage.org, 2019)

The current government is continuing its predecessor's prudent business-friendly policy framework and plans additional structural reforms that sustain Peru's economic competitiveness.

Some of the policies that have been continued or introduced are ideas such as formalizing the labor market, simplifying administrative procedures, and investing in infrastructure. Taxes for small businesses have been cut and regulations have been changed to allow easier registration of companies in regional government offices. Government corruption remains a serious problem. This factor limits foreign investor's confidence in the economy state-owned enterprises or SOEs remain active especially in the petroleum industry.

Trade is moderately important to Peru's economy. Value of imports and exports equals 45$% of GDP. Non-tariff barriers impede some trade.

Overall government policies do not significantly interfere with foreign investment.

The financial sector has undergone a gradual transformation. Credit in the private sector has increased and foreign ownership in the financial sector is growing.

3.2.2 *Chile*

Before the Spanish arrived in the sixteenth century, the Inca Indians controlled northern Chile while an indigenous group called the Mapuche lived in the central and southern part of Chile. Even though Chile proclaimed its independence in 1810 it was not able to defeat the Spanish until 1818. As time passed, Chile conquered Peru and Bolivia to gain its present northern region. Sometime during 1880, Chilean government secured control of the regions the Mapuche's held.

In more recent times Chile's history has encountered good and bad governments. Beginning in 1973, General Augusto Pinochet led a coup that overthrew Salvatore Allende's three-year-old Marxist government. While the Pinochet government was noted for some horrendous acts against its Chilean people it did implement sound economic policies, which were consistently maintained throughout the 1980s. Chilean citizens elected a democratically elected president in 1990, Patricio Aylwin. The implementation of well-developed practical economic policies contributed to steady growth and the decrease of poverty. These policies helped secure the country's commitment to democratic and representative government (www.infoplease, Chile, 2018).

3.3 Historical Perspective on Chile and Peru

3.3.1 *Peru*

Peru has a long rich history dating back to the years 1532–1533 when the Spanish conquistador Francisco Pizarro defeated the Incas. After some tumultuous events along the way and several military regimes, Peru eventually achieved a steady civilian government that began the economic development of Peru.

Between 1968 and 1980 the military again ruled Peru. Under General Juan Velasco Alvarado and in 1975 General Morales Bermudez. In 1980 Peru returned to civilian rule with the elected Fernando Belaunde However, all things are not well because the Sendero Luminoso or the Shining Path guerrillas began their protest and armed struggle. This was a communist revolution Party of Peru spreading Marxism, Leninism, and Maoism around the country. They wanted to overrule ruling class and install a communist regime. They were funded through narco-trafficking, ransoms, taxes on individuals and businesses. Thus began a decade and one-half fight trying to eradicate the military group.

In 1985, Alan Garcia Perez was elected President and began to reform the military and police. Because of misguided macroeconomic policies, the world economy, and just plain bad decisions, in 1988 Peru had to obtain assistance from the International Monetary Fund (IMF). Simultaneously, the Shining Path movement intensified. This caused significant turbulence among Peruvian citizens. Deaths, murders, and countryside terror were disrupting the normal way of life including economic development and business operations.

The 1990s began with the electing of center-right Alberto Fujimori as president. His platform was an appealing anti-corruption approach, budget austerity, and privatization process to reverse Peru's economic downward spin (Timeline 2012).

Major political restructuring was implemented with the supervision of the Peruvian constitution. During the same time the Shining Path's leader, Abimael Guzman is arrested, convicted, and sentenced to life in prison.

1993 brings a new constitution that is implemented, and Fujimori is re-elected. In 1994 Fujimori deals very forcefully with the Shining Path causing 6000 of its members to surrender. Another guerilla group emerged during this period. The Tupac Amara revolutionaries cause uproar and put Fujimori on the spot by forcing him to direct the Peruvian Special Forces to free hostages at the Japanese embassy. The internal turbulence with the Shining Path and the Tupac Amaru groups distracted the Peruvian electorate from pursuing the country's growth and development (Timeline 2012).

The year 2000 brings more bad news for President Fujimori. He is accused of human rights violations, kidnapping, and crimes against humanity among other political and financial problems one of which is treason.

With all the upheaval, an indigenous Stanford educated Peruvian economist Alejandro Toledo is elected President of Peru. Unfortunately,

Toledo's tenure was not as productive and successful as everyone thought it would be. His administration was accused of various scandals and other corrupt activity. Alejandro Toledo left office July 28, 2006. The lack of successful progress left him with a terribly low approval rating (Timeline 2012).

With Toledo leaving office it provided an opportunity for Alan Garcia to again come forward to be a candidate for President. No surprise, Garcia was elected again, and this time focused on ridding the country of drug trafficking and organized crime. He also advocated market economy and more aggressive macroeconomic approach to growing the economy.

During this time, Former President Fujimori faced a list of legal proceeding. He was tried and was convicted of a host of crimes which awarded him a 25-year prison sentence.

In President Garcia's second term (2006–2011) there was an average 7% GDP growth, a commodity boom, inflation was reduced to under 3%, and the percentage of Peruvian citizens in poverty fell from 48 to 28%. This was a dramatic change and a real positive accomplishment for the Garcia administration.

In 2011, Ollanta Mumala a Presidential candidate who offered the Peruvians social harmony and attention to inequality among Peru's citizens. His platform was attractive to the Peruvian people that led him to become Peru's President. During his term, he focused on the under privileged, respected the investor's rights, the rule of law and respect for the Peruvian constitution. President Ollanta Humala's term ended in July of 2016 (Peru Country Profile 2012).

In 2016, Pedro Pablo Kuczynski a 77-year-old liberal economist won the run-off election by a narrow margin. As an economist and former World Bank executive, Kuczynski brought economic policy thinking that could help the Peruvian economy continue its 5.9% growth rate. This growth was much better than other economies in the region. During his term in 2017 and 2018, President Kuczynski encountered political turmoil that created major economic uncertainty. Corruption emerged as one of the major issues causing concern among business and government officials. Kuczynski's admission of receiving advisory fees from Odebrecht a Brazilian construction company, while he was Peru's Minister of Economy and Finance, caused the Peruvian legislature to lose confidence in him and they moved toward impeachment. President Kuczynski resigned in March of 2018.

His successor Martin Viscarra became president. He has brought new hope and promise to the economy by encouraging investment (Country Profile—The Report: Peru 2018). It is hoped that President Viscarra can lead Peru to great success and continue its economic growth and development that has been its greatest achievement over the past decade.

3.3.2 Chile

Chile is about twice the size of Montana. It is located south of Peru, west of Bolivia and Argentina. It is located between the Andes mountain range and the Pacific Ocean. One-third of Chile is covered with the huge Andean mountain range in the North and the driest place on earth the Atacama Desert (Info please, 2018). Punta Arena is at the southernmost city in the world. Chile shares its border with three (3) countries, Peru, Bolivia, and Argentina. It is a Republic with a population of 17, 789, 267 citizens and a literacy rate of 97.5%.

An abbreviated chronology of Chile's development is listed below:

1970—Salvador Allende became the first democratically elected Marxist president of Chile. His administration introduced extensive programs of nationalization and radical social reforms.

1973—President Allende's chief of staff General Augusto Pinochet ousts President Allende from office in a coup and establishes a brutal dictatorship. This went on for almost 20 years.

1988—The Christian Democrats' Patricio Aylwin wins the presidential election and Pinochet steps down as chief of state but remains head of the army.

1994–1995—Edwardo Frei succeeds Alywin and reduces the military influence.

1998—General Pinochet retires from the army and is arrested in UK. Spain charges Pinochet with murder charges.

2000–2006—President Ricardo Lagos is elected in a run-off election.

2006—Michelle Bachelet is elected first woman President of Chile. During her term, Chile and China sign a free trade agreement.

2008—Tension with Peru and Chile regarding long-standing dispute over maritime territory.

2009—Military exercises again strain relations between Chile and Peru. Peruvian officer accused of spying for Chilean military.

2010—Sebastian Pinera defeats President Eduardo Frei in presidential elections (Chile Country Profile 2018).

3.4 Peru's Infrastructure

To meet the infrastructure needs by 2025, Peru has to invest approximately $160 billion dollars for the next decade. Throughout the country, there is a need for both private and public infrastructure amelioration. The areas of most concern include roads, telecommunication, ports, airports, water, sewage, health, and education (www.export.gov, construction, 2018).

One major and important development in the construction area is the arrangement of public, private partnerships (PPP). This was created by a legislative decree and is intended to facilitate the private investment to address all the infrastructure needs. The works for taxes law is stepping forward in asserting public/private programs for financing and implementing private projects that regional and local governments select (www.export.gov, construction, 2018). Peru has been ambitious and proactive in all areas of infrastructure investing not only in roads but in education, health care facilities, telecommunication, and water management projects. There is a prospering construction sector in Peru offering a wide variety of investment opportunities (www.export.gov, construction, 2018).

Peru's infrastructure gap has been widening as the country's economic growth has expanded. This has been a long-standing problem with chronic deficiencies in transport, energy, and industrial infrastructure.

Business investors have to face some infrastructure challenges when doing business in Peru. Peru ranks 89th globally for quality of infrastructure after Chile who is 44th, Mexico is 57th and Colombia is 84th. Peru's gap in infrastructure has been estimated at $160 billion dollars. To close the gap will require approximately 8.27% of national GDP. While it is a huge amount, it would pay big dividends and quickly increase GDP by 15.5% (Dettoni 2017).

Public officials have recognized the need to address these deficiencies however and have developed ambitious public–private partnerships (PPP) to meet the needs of these infrastructure requirements (Dettoni 2017).

Partnering with Investment Promotion agency ProInversion is an effective way to promote and accomplish the closing of the infrastructure gap. Since the new contracts associated with the PPPs have a very strong anti-corruption clause it is believed that the next version of ProInversion promotion efforts will be more efficient and effective by keeping projects structuring times within the 18–24 months or in line with the national standard (Dettoni 2017).

Table 3.1 Percent investment per project

Sector	*Percent invested*
Transportation	49.4
Education	13.5
Housing	5.6
Sanitation	10.3
Health	6.8
Agriculture & Irrigation	6.8
Streets and sidewalks	7.5
Total	100
Total amount	$9,015,982,359

Source https://www.export.gov/article?id=Peru-Construction-Equipment

This new effort will hopefully begin in the process of making the infrastructure projects work and begin closing the major infrastructure gaps that now exists in Peru. This will have a major impact on the growth and development of Peru. It will provide a major platform for international investors to invest. Continued improvement in infrastructure will have lasting positive effects on Peru's development.

3.4.1 *Projects*

Some of the most popular and needed projects include the following:

a. Metro line in Lima, Peru
b. Gas pipeline—one of the longest in Latin America
c. Jorge Chavez International Airport—$1.2 billion-dollar expenditure (Table 3.1).

3.4.2 *Chile's Infrastructure*

Chile has initiated a major infrastructure plan to revitalize its services and lead the country into a solid economic path. According to its leaders, Chile wants to modernize its transportation and health care systems. This will create jobs and fuel the economy (KPMG 2018). The Chilean government has established a $9 billion-dollar fund and an agency to administer the capital and work associated with a variety of infrastructure projects. The agency named Fondo de Infrastructure will be the controlling and directing agency in charge of infrastructure projects. This fund provides significant opportunities for investors with the PPP arrangement even more money $48 billion dollars through now to 2023 to complete 60 projects. The vision is to move Chile's transportation infrastructure into the twenty-first century. These projects will upgrade 24 significant highway projects and reduce chronic congestion on urban and interurban highways. Included in this infrastructure effort will be 18 hospital concessions and structures (KPMG 2018). Additionally, airports, ports, and public transit system will be enhanced. As such, Chile has many ambitious infrastructure projects that will enhance and strengthen the already strong economic situation Chile presents.

3.5 Business Trends in Peru

Peru's economy has been doing really well. Because of Peru's shining economic growth, there are lots of business opportunities. The beer market, tourism, and e-commerce are businesses that have demonstrated real potential in Peru.

Peru's geography lends itself to some very resourceful and profitable industries. The minerals found in the mountain regions have contributed to Peru's success in the mining industry and its affiliated businesses. Peru has a large and dynamic copper mining industry. With Peru's long coastline, the fishing and maritime industry have been able to flourish.

In another promising area, clothing and textile exports have been possible via the free trade agreements such as the Pacific Alliance and other world trading agreements with Europe and Asia. Since Peru has Alpaca herds, the fiber from their hair/fur can be used as a raw material in the production of various clothing products. Tourists like to purchase products produced from the Alpaca hair but tourists are not the only consumers of these products. The Peruvian nationals like the Alpaca products and purchase them as the trends frequently change (Investment in Peru 2017).

Investors need to be clear about the market and demand for clothing. The Pacific Alliance trading bloc has allowed Chile and Colombia to buy Peruvian goods without tariffs.

3.5.1 *Restaurants and Cafes*

In Peru well managed restaurants are profitable and very good businesses for the creation of wealth. Peruvians, traveling tourists, and people all over the world recognize the greatness of Peruvian cuisines.

The food industry is very competitive and as such, investors need to have a good analysis of location(s), segments, menus, promotion, and logistics -supply chain-(Investment in Peru 2017).

3.5.2 *Hotel and Guesthouses*

Tourist activity in Peru is significant. Approximately 4 million tourists visited Peru in 2017. Peru has incredible historic attractions that bring a huge number of people to the country. Again, potential investors need to do an in-depth analysis of locations, service availability, and infrastructure before making any serious investment (Investment in Peru 2017).

Website design—popular communication methods such as social media and other platforms have helped promote a variety of business ventures. Website design companies have flourished because of the need for businesses to reach a broad range of customers all over Peru, Latin America, and the world.

Entrepreneurs are working hard and continuously finding entrepreneurial opportunities due to the confidence in the Peruvian economy.

3.5.3 *E-Commerce*

E-commerce in Peru is a new market; however, interest across in Peru has increased steadily with 56% being the highest rate ever in Peru. The circumstances of high utilization of interest provide a great opportunity for e-commerce. The online marketplaces since 2015 have increased 70%. In store, sales have decreased approximately 5% as online sales surged 15–20%. The e-commerce in Peru is very impressive and growing. With the increased use of the Internet there is a sense that e-commerce will show continued growth. This is also due to the existence of continued economic growth in Peru's economy. Twenty-two percent of the users of the Internet in Peru have entered into a purchase online. In other shopping areas of e-commerce in Peru accessories and application 38%, technology 30% and clothing and footwear 30% all on the Internet (www.export.gov, Ecommerce, 2018).

3.5.4 *Mobile E-Commerce*

Among Latin American countries, Peru has the lowest smartphone utilization. It is projected that 10.1 million Peruvians will own a Smartphone by 2019. Presently the main approaches to the digital market in Peru are via (a) email, (b) social networking, and (c) search engine (SEO) and public search engines (www.export.gov, Ecommerce, 2018).

3.5.5 *Mining*

The proficient business and extraction practices among Peruvian companies have allowed Peru to achieve recognition as one of the largest mining producers in the world. Peru's enormous natural resource endowments combined with its easy entry and low startup costs make Peru an attractive destination for investment (Santarini 2017).

A Business startup is easy. Many companies like to invest in Peru because it is easy to do business there. There is easy market entry, easy company formation and easy company incorporation. Additionally, there are no restrictions on foreign stockholders. The incorporation process is simple and straight forward. Corporations and LLCs are the most popular business formations (Santarini 2017).

3.6 Business Trends in Chile

According to Roberts and Araujo (1997), Chile is an example of a country that has exploited entrepreneurship and innovation to establish and promote a rapidly expanding economy. Emerging from the depths of economic depression that engulfed the country several years ago, Chile has become a showcase of economic development. The strategic application of innovation and entrepreneurial policies in deregulating Chile's banking system is an example of new ideas benefiting the economy and society by bringing control back to the people. By modernizing the country's legal framework, the Chicago boys pushed private economic development as the main engine of growth. Because of the enormous effort to privatize, the role of the public sector has been reduced to an important supportive function, rather than the lead factor in decision-making. The public sector is now part of the team that sets the ground rules and maintains macroeconomics stability.

The Chilean trade commission has been very aggressive over the years in campaigning for Chile to the world. Pro Chile has 35 offices world-wide pushing Chile building interest, business relationships and developing international trade. It has a huge amount of information on the important and popular industry in Chile.

3.6.1 *Telecommunication*

Chile's telecommunication infrastructure is probably the most modern and developed system in Latin America. However, even with this state of telecommunication, Chile still has to invest more to close the digital gap in telecommunication. Over the next four years, Chile plans to augment its investment in telecommunication by 30%.

In the same general area, Mobile telephones and broadband sectors are growing faster than any other telecommunication sector in Chile (www.export.gov, telecommunication, 2018).

3.6.2 *Education and Training*

Chile has a program entitled "Becas Chile". This educational incentive program provides scholarships to post-grad students and internships for technical graduates. In 2018 the program focused on the challenging areas such as water resources, digital transformation, and resilience to disaster of natural origin.

Presently 40% of 18–24-year olds are enrolled in higher education (www.export.gov, Chile, Education training, 2018).

3.7 Discussion

Both Chile and Peru have very rich histories. They are both rich in landscape and in culture that has been part of their external environment for centuries. While this richness is abounding, their histories have not always been rosy. Peru's rocky decades of the 1960s and 1970s and the Shining Path scandals of the Fujimori administration created some major concerns over time.

Similarly, the Allende and Pinochet regimes in Chile brought about a lot of anger and suffering among the Chilean population. Some of the scars of both countries' ugly histories are still in many of the citizens of those countries. Paradoxically, in during the Pinochet era economic freedom and political terror coexisted. Fortunately, the political terror went away, and the economic freedom remained and have become the basis for the strong economy that Chile presents today. Similarly, in Peru during the Fujimori regime, the economy grew while democracy was left to shrink and decline. Fortunately, the economic and political stability that exists in each country today is welcomed and good for the citizens and their children. Both countries have come a long way in transforming their economies and societies. Both countries have learned that economic and political stability is much better for increasing the quality of life than what existed under the Pinochet and Fujimori regimes.

3.8 Conclusion

When reviewing country economic and political performance over the last two decades, Chile and Peru have continued to make the correct policy decisions. Chile especially has had an enormously successful run over this time period. As mentioned many times before Chile has become the showcase economy among Latin American countries with indications of getting better and better. Peru has shown very good and positive signs also. There have been some ups and downs especially with the corruption issues associated with former President Pedro Pablo Kuczyinski and his bribery scandal and the Obredecht involvement of former Peruvian presidents. Even with these distractions, as bad as they are with regard to the country's reputation, Peru continues to recover and has been able to initiate and implement good economic and political policies under the Presidency of Martin Vizcarra. Peru seems to be back on the path to a growing stable economy and more responsive political environment. Hopefully, this situation will continue between both Chile and Peru for the long-term future.

3.8.1 Case Example of Business in Chile

Vigatec is a company founded in Chile, South America in 1980. This company is based in Santiago, Chile with branches located in Ecuador, Bolivia, and Brazil. It is an SME with about 200 employees. Vigatec is in the technology business. The company is involved in several business activities such as (a) reselling and marketing plastic cards, (b) mail handling equipment, (c) control and security systems, and (d) packaging equipment.

This company is another example of an enterprise that established itself in Chile, took advantage of the good business environment and progressively grew and became more sophisticated in its product lines and managerial skills (Vigatec 2019).

References

Chile. https://www.infoplease.com/world/countries/chile. Accessed November 20, 2018.

Chile Country Profile. 2018. BBC News. https://www.bbc.com/news/world-latin-america-19357497. Accessed December 10, 2018.

Chile Profile—Timeline. 2017. www.bbc.com/news/world-latin-america-19356356.

Country Profile—The Report: Peru. 2018. https://oxfordbusinessgroup.com/peru-2018/country-profile. Accessed January 26, 2019.

Dettoni, Jacopo. 2017. Peru Looks to PPPs to Solve Infrastructure Woes. http://www.fdiintelligence.com/Location/Americas/Peru/Peru-looks-to-PPP-to-solve-infrastructure-woes. Accessed February 19, 2019.

Export.Gov. 2018. https://www.export.gov/article?id=Peru-Agricultural-Sectors.

https://www.export.gov/article?id=Peru-Construction-Equipment.

https://www.export.gov/article?id=Peru-Education.

https://www.export.gov/article?id=Peru-Food-Processing-Packaging-Equipment.

https://www.export.gov/article?id=Peru-ECommerce.

https://www.export.gov/article?id=Peru-Joint-Ventures.

https://www.export.gov/article?id=Chile-Telecommunications-Sector.

https://www.export.gov/article?id=Chile-Automotive-Parts.

https://www.export.gov/article?id=Chile-Market-Entry-Strategy.

https://www.export.gov/article?id=Chile-Agricultural-Machinery-and-Equipment.

https://www.export.gov/article?id=Chile-Education-and-Training.

https://www.heritage.org/index/country/peru, 2019 Index of Economic Freedom.

https://www.cia.gov/library/publications/the-world-factbook/geos/print_ci.html.

https://www.export.gov/article?id=Peru-Franchising. Accessed March 14, 2019.

https://www.export.gov/article?id=Peru-Market-Challenges. Accessed March 13, 2019.

Investments in Peru. 2017. Investments in Peru: These Are the Most Profitable Businesses. https://peru.info/en-us/business/news/5/23/these-are-the-most-profitable-businesses-in-peru. Accessed January 26, 2019.

Katz, Lothar. 2007. *Negotiating International Business*, 2nd ed. Charleston: Booksurge Publishing.

Katz, Lothar. 2017. *Negotiating International Business: Negotiations Reference Guide to 50 Countries Around the World*. Charleston: Booksurge Publishing.

KPMG. 2018. http://home.Kpmg/xx/en/home/insights/2018/11/investments-raises-chile-infrastructure.html. Accessed February 19, 2019.

Peru Country Profile. 2012. http://news.bbc.co.uk/2/hi/americas/country_profiles/1224656.stm. Accessed January 13, 2019.

Peru Country Review. 2018. Country Watch. http://www.countrywatch.com.

Peru: Doing Business Report-Peru Enacts Reforms to Improve Business Climate, Asia News Monitor, Bangkok, November 2018. http://search.proquest.com/abicomplete/docview/2130143486/BB45Df3B624893PQ/1?accountid=13153. Accessed March 15, 2019.

Roberts, P.C., and K.L. Araujo. 1997. *The Capitalist Revolution in Latin America*. New York: Oxford University Press.

Santarini, Maria. 2017. Why Choose to Do Business in Peru? BizLatin Hub. http://www.bizlatinhub.com/do-business-peru/. Accessed March 15, 2019.

Srinivasan, Mandyam M., Theodore P. Stank, Philippe-Pierre Dornier, and Kenneth J. Petersen. 2014. *Global Supply Chains: Evaluating Regions on an EPIC Framework—Economy Politics, Infrastructure, and Competence*. New York: McGraw-Hill.

Timeline. 2012. Timeline: Peru—"A Chronology of Key Events". http://news.bbc.co.uk/2/hi/Americas/country-profiles/1224690.stm. Accessed January 13, 2019.

Vigatec. 2019. http://www.viartec.com.ar/vigatec.php. Accessed April 19, 2019.

CHAPTER 4

Cultural Issues Affecting Business Activity in Chile and Peru

4.1 Introduction

Cultural considerations in business decisions and transactions are significant. Not only do these considerations affect the individual employees, but they also affect the functional areas of the business. One critical area that culture influences is whether to enter a new market or not. Companies that continue to enter the global market place have to seriously think about training their employees to deal with culture. Cross-cultural teams have to have diverse knowledge and insightful approaches to the challenges of business. Some of the primary areas of concern relate to communication, etiquette, and organizational structure.

People have to understand that workplace differences require different behaviors. Formality may be more important than casualty in different places in the world. These attributes require different responses. In Chile and Peru, punctuality has a different definition than in other parts of the world. Values and norms that exist in one country do not exist in another. Chile and Peru have the same language and, in some cases, the same heritage but by and large Chile is quite different than Peru.

Considering the entire culture of both Chile and Peru is very important before any business development is considered.

J. E. Spillan and M. N. Rahman, *Doing Business in Chile and Peru*,
https://doi.org/10.1007/978-3-030-25073-7_4

4.2 Background

Culture is the most complex variable that businesses operating in the international arena have to understand. Because culture is composed of norms, values beliefs, and customs. Business people need to know how these factors affect consumers attraction to product and service offerings (Wild and Wild 2019).

Besides the regular items of discussion about beliefs, values, etc., business people need to understand the national culture, the subcultures and the physical environment (Wild and Wild 2019). A national culture is built and sustained when a country preserves its legacy by building museums, erecting statues, and presenting traditional events. These cultural attractions manifest the obvious importance of the culture and show the world its uniqueness as a country and its people. The subcultures are also important because the people of these cultural subsets possess different and unique attributes that can have a major impact on product/service marketing and day to day operations of a business. An example of this is in China where there are 50 distinct ethnic groups. Decision about product design, packaging, and advertising need to consider each group's distinct cultural characteristics. Marketing companies need to reflect different language dialects and idioms (Wild and Wild 2019).

The physical environment also has an impact on personal communication in a culture.

As Fig. 4.1 presents, culture is a very complex construct with several very complex constructs embedded in its core. All cultures have these elements and in some cultures the complexities are more substantive than others. The personal communication part of this map includes language which is in itself a very involved part of culture and can shape understandings of different aspects of culture in different ways. The bottom line is that culture is complex, not easy to understand, and is a critical factor in the success of any business development in any global environment.

4.3 Social Structure

Social structure is a culture's fundamental organization which consists of groups, institutions with its systems of social positions, and relationships along with the way resources are allocated (Wild and Wild 2019).

Social structures play an important role in various aspects of business such as production, site selection, advertising, methods, and cost of doing

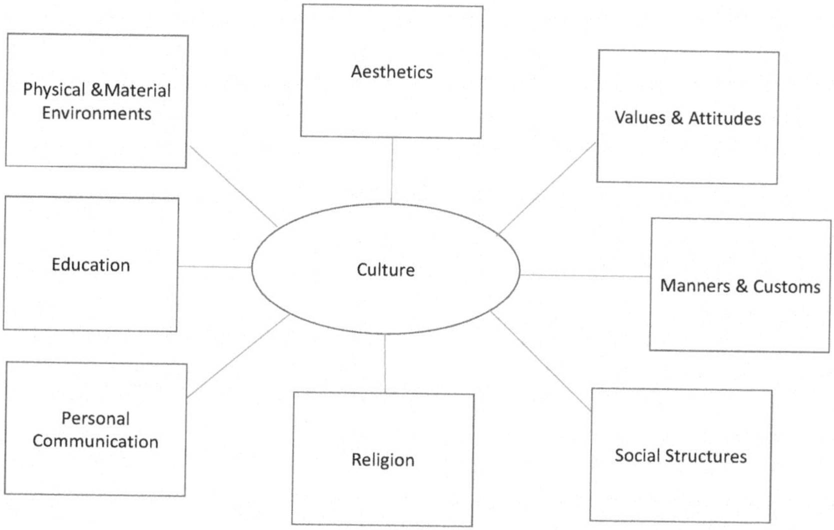

Fig. 4.1 Components of culture (*Source* Adapted from Wild and Wild [2019, page 45])

business in the foreign country. Both family and gender are important factors in consumer behavior, and therefore need to be understood so that the company's business model focuses on the appropriate target market for their products and services.

In social structures and social status there is a concept called social stratification. This idea relates to social status by classifying people based on family heritage, income, and occupation (Wild and Wild 2019).

Social mobility is another dimension of social structure that is part of culture. The movement from one class level to another is easy in some cultures and difficult in others. In today's world the class system and cast system are the primary social status groupings (Wild and Wild 2019).

4.4 Religion

Values emanate from religious beliefs. Each religious denomination has a different view of the world, work, savings, and materials. As such, these ideas are predominating in the business world and thus have an impact on how consumer behavior is affected. Depending on the geographical location of an international company, the religion of that country may have an impact on the business relationship, the managerial styles, and the marketing activities that operate in the company (Wild and Wild 2019).

4.4.1 Language

With the pervasiveness of the Internet along with the multiple platforms for communication the Internet provides, i.e. Facebook, Twitter, Google Mail, etc., companies are faced with incredible challenges trying to keep pace with social media exchanges. These are important areas for companies to become intricately involved because across the globe customers announce their tastes, preferences, and buying habits online and anticipate an enjoyable buying experience. E-commerce has become the rule rather than the exception. As such, being able to understand the different languages around the globe is essential for understanding consumer needs, tastes, and buying habits.

4.5 Cultural Characteristics

One of the main differences in doing business abroad versus doing business domestically is the cultural variable. No one variable has such an important impact on the business activities and decision outcomes as the issue of culture.

Culture relates to one's beliefs, values, customs, and thoughts. It is the primary way that people's thoughts and mindsets are developed in a society. Culture is learned not innate. All people are socialized into the beliefs and customs of the society in which they are born. Such things as time span, attitudes, symbols, religion, education, and social structure are all important parts of culture that are learned from birth to adulthood. Language is and continues to be a central part of culture. While English is widespread in the Western world and growing in the East, it is the one cultural variable that can make or break a business negotiation or transaction (Cavusgil et al. 2017).

Culture relates to how its members live, how they dress, how they speak, how they eat, and how they think. Culture determines a person's behavior and his/her mindsets. The people living in the mountains and the valleys hold on to various methods and customs of living. Their product and service needs are different from those who live in a metropolitan area. The use of computers and high-speed Internet in the Andes highlands among the indigenous dwelling is limited due to the remoteness of their dwellings and the size of their meager budgets. Climate in these areas and coldness in the mountains and nearness to the sea all have a major impact on the way businesses conduct their marketing and sales operation (Wild and Wild 2019).

4.5.1 *Workplace and Culture*

People/workers are affected by the country's culture, norms, customs, and way of life impact the way people come to work, their work behavior and the methods they use to complete their work assignments. Essentially, culture affects workers view of work. For example, for the French, work is a means to an end while in the United States work is an end in itself. Culture many times requires companies to adjust their business policies and practices. This sometimes becomes known as situational management. Companies may be required to change comply with the local culture. As such, the managers in foreign environments must take a long view of the culture they are working in and be patient (Wild and Wild 2019).

International business and culture are intricately tied. Culture is a determining variable when it comes to doing business in a foreign country. Knowing a country's culture and how to adapt to it while building a business is a foreign country can be a tricky exercise (Cavusgil et al. 2017).

4.6 Culture and International Business

Cross-cultural relationships and interactions have an impact on business activity among companies and countries. Company managers have to have a level of empathy and tolerance. Additionally, they need accurate factual knowledge about the culture to effectively compete and successfully manage marketing, production and full operations of the company in a foreign environment. To be successful a company administration must understand the cultural context as it relates to:

- Managing employees
- Communication and interacting with foreign associates
- Negotiating and developing international ventures
- Developing products and services
- Preparing all advertising and promotional information
- Evaluating and selecting foreign distributors

- Interfacing with current or potential foreign customers (Cavusgil et al. 2017).

Most companies have a distinctive corporate culture. This corporate culture determines how the employees and administration operates and transacts business internally and externally. The interface between the company's culture and the country's national culture can produce a variety of challenges for managers.

Within this context, managers have to think about and be careful not to risk an ethnocentric orientation, where the company manager uses their own culture for judging other cultures. Ethnocentric orientated managers believe that their own race, religion, or ethnic group is superior to others. There is a tendency to be ethnocentric, however, managers who are effective and successful actively avoid this orientation. They generally adopt a polycentric or geocentric orientation. Polycentric meaning that the local area or region attachment is adopted while geocentric means a global mindset where managers can understand the respective culture and adapt without regard to country or borders (Cavusgil et al. 2017). The key to being successful in foreign environments is to keep an open mind with a curious attitude that does not judge or make conclusions about others' behavior. Training that focuses on people watching skills and human relations skills will be transferred across borders. Periodic training sessions that update managers and employees using simulations and case studies are important to assist managers in meeting cross-cultural challenges (Cavusgil et al. 2017).

4.6.1 *Cultural Orientation*

The name Chile is derived from the native Ymara word Chilli meaning "the land where the earth ends". Chile is thought of as the most homogeneous country in Latin America in ethnically and culturally. Chile does not have a problem with regional identities. However, there are still regional trends and traditions that do exist. The areas near Bolivia, Aymara Indians have preserved major parts of their Andean culture. In the south the Mapuche indigenous areas large culture that contributed significantly to the Chilean culture.

The Chilean culture has been influenced and formed by the arrival of large groups of immigrants from Germany, Britain, France, Italy, Croatia, Palestine, and Jews. These immigrants have risen to become influential in political and business positions (Countries and Their Cultures 2019).

Food has a special place in Chilean culture. Chilean cuisines have been influenced by both Indian and European factors.

Climate also plays an important role in the construction of the natural culture identity. Most Chileans are of mixed ancestry and the country has a high degree of homogeneity which has prevented conflicts among the Chilean people. The climate varies from north to south and in some instances to extremes.

Chileans are quite nationalistic and patriotic. They are accustomed to national leaders and members from the intellectual elites without Spanish surnames, i.e. presidents with French name like Pinochet (Countries and Their Cultures 2019).

4.7 National Culture and Subcultures and Communication

4.7.1 Peru Culture

Culture many times is neglected in developmental plans. Essentially policymakers neglect cultural factors because realistically there are no accurate measurements available. To most people culture seems to be a vague idea (Whyte 1963).

Peru has a surplus of unskilled workers and a shortage of skilled workers. A blue-collar worker is called Orebro and a white-collar worker is called an empleado. Both of these terms denote a social class demarcation. Being an Orebro is less status than an empleado. When questioned some Peruvians said that they would not be an Obrero under any circumstances.

Trust is another issue that is culturally driven. Most organizations need a certain level of trust among the employees to accomplish the daily tasks. Peruvians generally lack the trust that essentially brings the organizational parts together to become functionally effective. This attribute, trust, is necessary for delegation of duties. Faith in the trustworthiness of employees is critical. Without trust and faith in one's ability then managers rely on micro management practices which are inefficient and most of the time ineffective (Whyte 1963) (Fig. 4.2).

The Machu Picchu Inca civilization remains that is presented in the foregoing picture has become a very popular tourist visiting place for decades. Set high in the Andes Mountains, it sits above the Urubamba River valley. It is a relic of the fifteenth century. The Inca Indians built this sophisticated structure with incredible stone walls composed of huge finely carved stone.

Fig. 4.2 Machu Picchu—Great Inca civilization remains (*Source* https://www.pexels.com/search/machu%20picchu/, 2019)

The engineering and intricate structure of the walls, inclines, and levels is absolutely remarkable. It is hard to believe that such engineering thought existed in the fifteenth century. It is just an amazing site to visit and study for an understanding of the ancient Inca empire. Because Machu Picchu is such an intense experience many times foreigners associate the entire Peruvian culture with what they see at this site.

Peruvian Communication Styles
When speaking the Peruvians use the "Usted" or formal introduction form of communication. This is a gesture of respect. This form of expression is especially popular in the altiplano area or Andean populations which have been slow to change. This formal style has been shifting and in contemporary Peru, especially in the middle and upper classes and in large cities like Lima the "Tu" or informal has become the ordinary or an indication of modernity (Peru: Culture 2019).

In the nonverbal categories, the handshake is the most customary approach for greeting people. For men it is usual for them to touch the person with their left hand. This is generally among men. The introduction of men or women ordinarily comes with a kiss to each other on the cheek. While these approaches are normal among urban people, they are not generally the norm among Andean people. The people of this region like handshaking and a hug.

Peruvians are normally soft-spoken people because they have respect for their neighbor or the person(s) next to them.

In the first instance, Peruvians are not direct. They many times refrain from making their point until they have established a good relationship with the person they are communicating with or for whom business is being transacted. After a relationship has been established, then much more direct communication is developed (Peru: Culture 2019).

Attire

By and large, Peruvians dress with the intention of making a good impression. No matter what their societal status, Peruvians put the best mark on their physical presentation. Peruvians normally dress formally for work. They respect the work environment and the people that are in those settings, hence they want to abide by the etiquettes of the workplace.

Punctuality

Many times, Latins get a bad rap for not respecting time. In Peru punctuality is an important aspect of work life. Even though it is many times difficult to get to work on time because of the lack of modern transportation systems in Peru, most Peruvians try very hard to achieve the work punctuality requirements. In many business environments, being late to work carries serious penalties with some infractions leading to termination (Peru: Culture 2019).

Mutual Salutation

Peruvian's are very respectful people. They are generally informal in the salutation of co-workers by calling one another by their first names. It is different if there is a formal meeting with external people. These situations require the workers to address each other by formal names such as Senor, Doctor, Ingeniero. Respecting each other is a theme running through the Peruvian business culture.

Gender Equality
Peru is a complicated society. History has shaped many of the innate views of many people of Peru. History has also created some very rigid social class stratifications. With a large indigenous population, tension and friction has been a constant among the Peruvian population. The people of Criollo ethnicity have established themselves at the top of the social and political hierarchy and hence better than the others. This circumstance has influenced the workplace relationships not only in work interactions but also in recruiting, selecting, and hiring Peruvian people (Peru: Culture 2019).

Religion
Freedom of religion is a given in Peru. Roman Catholicism is the primary denomination in Peru. A variety of evangelical churches have become very popular among the Peruvian population. Along with the formal denominational religions, native tribes with rural backgrounds have different views of religion and worship traditions. While some of these have been marginalized, they are still practiced in many of the Andean and rural regions of Peru (Peru: Culture 2019).

4.7.2 Chile

Communication
By and large, Chileans are direct in their communications. However, Chileans frequently are indirect and use many nonverbal communication mechanisms to relay their message(s). In the workplace a Chilean employee may take more time than would be normal to respond to requests from a manager. Eye contact, smiling, and other body language cues can be messages that are not openly presented but send a signal about the employees' reaction to a manager request or comment.

Chileans enjoy a lively energetic conversation when they are having fun with friends and acquaintances. They use gestures and various methods are employed to persuade or convince another person on a particular perspective or point of view (Chile: Culture 2019).

Social Interactions
There seems to be a transition going on in the Chilean culture where the older Chilean society members are focused on caring and concerning about other people where the younger Chileans appear to have more concentration on success or personal gains.

Work Environment

Formal dress is generally required in the work environment. People recognize authority and the hierarchy. This is many times expressed in the way a person is dressed. Poor dress on both men and women side is frowned upon (Chile: Culture 2019).

Punctuality

Punctuality in the work environment is expected. Not respecting the time for work and its beginning and end points is not a good value for a Chilean. However, Chileans accept as normal that people are fifteen to twenty minutes late for a dinner or party.

Introductions/Salutations

Introductions are identical to those described for Peruvians. Normally, Chileans require the introductions to be formal with an exchange of formal names rather than first name. This can change if the Chilean wants his/her first name used. Once the initial introduction is consummated and the people are of the same age, generation and education they will address each other by their first name. Older people are addressed by their professional title or their formal title, i.e. Mr. Mrs. Or Miss. Exchange of business cards is an easy way to expedite and accurately communicate introductions (Chile: Culture 2019).

Chileans recognize attributes that are related to being an accomplished person. They admire people having high levels of education, and experience. While Chilean managers are generally conservative, they normally like open-mindedness. Many times, employees are open to nontraditional ways of doing things and that people who are not from the company's geographic area might not understand the process or corporate culture. Chileans are flexible and amenable to making the learning process as easy as possible for those who are not accustomed to the company's ways of doing business.

Gender and Work

Women have a slim disadvantage in the Chilean workplace just because of the machismo ethic. Men continue to dominate in the decision-making, however, fortunately things are changing as more women enter the workforce. Women have the same educational opportunities as men and increasingly women are foregoing various aspects of their life to follow a professional career. Women who are successful professionally are highly respected by men and women (Chile: Culture 2019).

Religion
Roman catholicism is the primary religion in Chile. While there have been some shifts in people's attitudes and beliefs the Catholic Church seems to reign supreme in Chile. Change among young people is having an impact on the Catholic Church in Chile.

The Catholic Church has a straight-line relationship with governments and opposition members. To be candid, the Catholic Church has experienced some serious turbulence over the years and has not retained the absolute allegiance of all Chileans (Chile: Culture 2019).

Class and Ethnicity
Chile is a country of definite and strict economic and social classes. Presently there are increasing inequalities between the higher and lower income sectors. The upper middle class are essentially in control of the finances and resources of the country. These people are generally well educated and are descendants of successful people who have a long history in Chile. Their families are heavily involved in private education.

The middle class is comprised of the professionals, small business owners, and other people of modest income levels. This group represents the bulk of the Chilean population.

By and large a person's social status is determined by his or her family name. Rural areas present even more pronounced division in class levels (Chile: Culture 2019).

Overall, personal relationships among colleagues and clients are of utmost importance in business and working environments. Establishing a rapport and solid trusting relationship is critical to successful business in Chile.

4.8 Education—Peru and Chile

4.8.1 Peru Education

Peru has compulsory education in almost all schools that include primary and secondary schools. These schools accommodate children from 5 to 16 years old. In the urban sections of Peru like Lima, Trujillo, Chimbote, etc. the children usually enter and complete the first two levels of school—primary and secondary. The school time and length are 30 hours a week or approximately 183 days per year.

These schools follow a national curriculum for all levels of education. By and large most educational instruction is done in Spanish, however in some rural areas classes are delivered in Aymara and Quechua as the language of instruction.

This compulsory school education is not always the case. In the altiplano or Andes region and the interior Amazon region many children do not attend school for a variety of reasons, i.e. poverty (children have to work), lack of resources to staff the schools. It is more often that children do not go to school in these geographic areas.

Unfortunately, over the years the number of students attending schools has been declining.

Peru has vocational schools which are classified into three categories: (a) technological, (b) teacher training, and (c) arts. Finally, Peru has a higher education system that is comprised of two segments. There are 51 Public Universities and 89 Private Universities. Public Universities are free while the Private Universities require substantial tuition. For-profit universities are becoming more popular across the country, causing alarm among seasoned educators. They worry about the quality and cost of education the for-profit universities delivery to its students. The government has passed legislation to require inspection of for-profit and other universities to evaluate the quality that is being delivered to the students attending these institutions (Clark 2015).

Figure 4.3 shows a typical school classroom that is seen across Latin America especially in the altiplano. While many of the schools in Peru's metropolitan areas such as Lima, Trujillo, and Chimbote are more modern, the Andes highlands still have a primitive society look. The indigenous populations have changed little over the centuries carrying on the customs and ways of life of the ancient Inca civilizations. From modern Western standards, this school setting is very primitive.

The human development index life expectancy, education, and per capita income indicators, which are used to rank countries into four tiers of human development. As one can see Peru's human development index is OK but could be significantly improved with better education in the Altiplano Andes or rural areas of the country. Table 4.1 shows the trends over a 10 year period 2007–2017. It has been growing at an annual rate of 0.64% (World Data Atlas, 2018, https://knoema.com/atlas/Peru).

The adult literacy rate in Peru is 94.17%. That is a very good rate when we compare it to the United States which has a literacy rate of 99% (World Data Atlas, 2018, https://knoema.com/atlas/Chile).

Fig. 4.3 Typical school classroom found across Latin America in the altiplano areas (*Source* Personal photo of inside a typical classroom seen across Latin America)

Table 4.1 Human development ranking 2007–2017

Date	*Value*	*Change (%)*
2017	0.75	0.26
2016	0.75	0.37
2015	0.75	−0.11
2014	0.75	1.30
2013	0.74	0.96
2012	0.73	−0.02
2011	0.73	1.73
2010	0.72	0.33
2009	0.71	0.34
2008	0.71	1.37
2007	0.70	1.07

Source World Data Atlas, 2018, https://knoema.com/atlas/Peru

4.8.2 Chile Education

As in Peru, Chile has compulsory education for all Chileans. Its education system has five core levels consisting of preschool, primary school, secondary school, and technical education.

The preschools are open to children up to 5 years old. The primary school education is open to children from 5 to 13 years and the secondary education is open to those children from 13 to 18 years of age. The technical/vocational or professional education provides an education continuum that consists of vocational training such as metal assembly, electrical training, and mechanical studies which prepare the student for professional or craft-man type jobs.

The Chilean government provides funding for children's schooling if they are unable to pay for private schooling. While the government finances the public schools, it also can fund private schools.

The University system requires all students to try a University selection exam. There are two exams which determine selection of students and the area of interest that each student wants to pursue (Education in Chile 2019).

Historically, Chilean Universities have been known as being among the best in Latin America. Chile has 25 State Universities, and many private universities (Atlantic Council 2019).

The human development index life expectancy, education, and per capita income indicators, which are used to rank countries into four tiers of human

Table 4.2 Human development ranking 2007–2017

Date	*Value*	*Change (%)*
2017	0.84	0.16
2016	0.84	0.23
2015	0.84	0.78
2014	0.83	0.60
2013	0.83	1.17
2012	0.82	0.57
2011	0.81	0.73
2010	0.81	0.45
2009	0.80	−0.20
2008	0.81	1.44
2007	0.79	0.85

Source World Data Atlas, 2018, https://knoema.com/atlas/Chile

development. As one can see Peru has a relatively high human development index. Table 4.2 shows the trends over a 10 year period 2007–2017. It has been growing at an annual rate of 0.64% (World Data Atlas, 2018, https://knoema.com/atlas/Chile).

The adult literacy rate in Chile is 96.63%. That is a very good rate when we compare it to the United States which has a literacy rate of 99% (World Data Atlas, 2018, https://knoema.com/atlas/Chile).

4.9 Discussion

There is a very important relationship between a country's culture and its formulation of business strategies. The consequences of discounting culture can be significant. The country's culture determines the mood or atmosphere in which a business will be operating. Customers and attributes are hard to erase and hence business investors have to consider these characteristics in the business development process and the business planning process. Belief and value systems are important parts of a business organization. Attitudes about business and how businesses operate is fundamentally defined by the culture in which it operates. Culture will be a determining factor in what goods and services are offered. Culture determines the work ethic and motivations of the workforce. Taking into consideration all of these cultural concerns is a difficult task. It is much more difficult than accounting for the finances of a business or building the brick and mortar structure. It requires real study of the cultural attributes and what elements of the culture are going to have an impact on the business's operation, performance, and its success.

4.10 Conclusion

While Chile and Peru have acquired many of the characteristics of businesses in developed countries, they still have a great many cultural attributes that are so deeply embedded in their culture that business investors many times do not understand. Any misunderstanding can create havoc and major challenges. On the other hand, understanding the local culture can not only provide a company or investor with a good understanding of the customer's desires and needs but also this knowledge gives the firm a greater competitive advantage. Being knowledgeable of a country's culture can allow the business investor to be a better marketer, negotiator, and all-around manager. To be successful in Chile and Peru's business environments business investors and managers need to thoroughly understand the cultures that exist in these countries.

Business Examples
The following presents some successful businesses that have been established in Peru and Chile over the years have demonstrated success to its owners, employees, community, and country:

Credicorp (BAP)
Peru
BAP has a substantial holding in the Peruvian financial market. It has a strong commercial banking, insurance, and pension fund operation that is available to all sectors of the population. BAP is well recognized and securely positioned with the banking and investment community of Latin America. It has helped its customers grow and develop which has ultimately contributed to the economic and social well-being of the Peruvian region, its community and the people who live in Peru. It is a company with strong leadership and continuous growth. The company's portfolio has multiplied 15 times in the last 22 years even when the global markets and financial turmoil was occurring. This company is an excellent example of how well managed companies can be a success to itself and to the Peruvian people (BAP 2019).

Chile

Televisión Nacional de Chile (TVN) is a Chilean public broadcasting company. Eduardo Frei Montalva founded the company in 1969. After the initial opening of the business, the company was reorganized on several occasions and its operations areas have increased over the years, becoming one of the leading television broadcasters in Chile and South America. Its home office is in Santiago and has a workforce of approximately 1083 employees. TVN is the only public Television company in Chile and has to compete for its audiences with the other private broadcasters that exist in Chile. Good example of a public company that has to maintain quality service to keep it competitive edge (TVN 2019).

References

Atlantic Council. 2019. https://www.atlanticcouncil.org/?view=article&id=18431:chile-best-education-system, accessed January 25, 2019.

BAP. 2019. https://credicorp.gcs-web.com/, accessed April 27, 2019.

Cavusgil, Tamer S., Gary Knight, and John R. Riesenberger. 2017. *International Business: New Realities*, 4th ed. New York: Pearson.

Chile: Culture. 2019. https://www.international.gc.ca/cil-cai/country_insights-apercus_pays/ci-ic_cl.aspx?lang=eng. https://globaledge.msu.edu/countries/chile/culture, accessed April 6, 2019.

Chile—Guide to Language, Culture, Customs and Etiquette. 2019. https://www.commisceo-global.com/resources/country-guides/chile-guide, accessed April 6, 2019.

Clark, Nick. 2015. Education-in-Peru, http://wenr.wes.org/2015/04/education-in-peru, accessed April 6, 2017.

Countries and Their Cultures—Forum. 2019. http://www.everyculture.com/bo-co/Chile.html.

Education in Chile. 2019. https://www.studycountry.com/guide/CL-education.htm.

https://knoema.com/atlas/Chile/Corruption-perceptions-index, accessed April 14, 2019.

https://knoema.com/atlas/Peru/Adult-literacy-rate, accessed April 14, 2019.

https://knoema.com/atlas/Peru, accessed April 14, 2019.

https://knoema.com/atlas/Chile, accessed April 14, 2019.

https://www.pexels.com/search/machu%20picchu/, 2019.

https://stock.adobe.com/images/group-of-children-heading-to-school-in-the-morning-wearing-colorful-traditional-clothing-walking-down-the-street-in-school-uniforms-in-cusco-peru/216078963?as_ channel=affiliate&as_campaign=pexels&as_source=arvato&tduid=93de7442b1c465f101bb149cc2d3f875&as_channel=affiliate&as_campclass=redirect&as_source=arvato.

Peru: Culture. 2019. https://globaledge.msu.edu/search?q=Peruvian+culture#gsc.tab=0&gsc.q=Peruvian%20culture&gsc.page=1, accessed April 6, 2019.

TVN. 2019. https://www.youtube.com/channel/UCRyluqJAMMrdGgz-uQdFt7w/about?disable_polymer=1, accessed April 27, 2019.

Whyte, William F. 1963. Culture, Industrial Relations, and Economic Development: The Case of Peru. *ILR Review* 15 (4): 583–594.

Wild, John J., and Kenneth L. Wild. 2019. *International Business: The Challenges of Globalization*, 9th ed. New York: Pearson.

CHAPTER 5

The Political Climate

5.1 Introduction

Political climate in Chile and Peru is far from being stable. However, the business community always finds a way to adjust to the situation. This Chapter provides a descriptive picture of the political climate of Chile and Peru, with reference to how it affects conducting business in the respective country. This chapter also provided detail insight into the overall political climate, issues such as regional politics, transparency, political risk, and legal system. This chapter provides detailed analysis of obstacle to entrepreneurship. This chapter also provides information about how contracts and agreements are documented.

5.2 Background

5.2.1 Chile

When the democratic government led by Aylwin took over from the military during the early 1990s Chile made a strong case as an economic role model in the world (Clinton 2011). According to the World Bank data, Chile sustained a growth averaging 4% per year since 1999. Chile also deepened its long-standing commitment to trade liberalization with the signing of a free trade agreement with the United States in 2004 (USTR.gov). Chile claims to have more bilateral or regional trade agreements than any other country. It has 57 such agreements, including with the European

J. E. Spillan and M. N. Rahman, *Doing Business in Chile and Peru*,
https://doi.org/10.1007/978-3-030-25073-7_5

Union, Mercosur, China, India, South Korea, and Mexico (WTO). Over the past seven years, foreign direct investment inflows have quadrupled to some $15 billion in 2010, but FDI had dropped to about $7 billion in 2009 in the face of diminished investment throughout the world based on World Bank data. The Chilean government conducts a rule-based countercyclical fiscal policy, accumulating surpluses in sovereign wealth funds during periods of high copper prices and economic growth, and allowing deficit spending only during periods of low copper prices and growth. Those sovereign wealth funds—kept mostly outside the country and separate from Central Bank reserves—amounted to more than $20 billion. Chile used $4 billion from this fund to finance a fiscal stimulus package to fend off recession. Chile to become a full member of OECD in 2009. In May 2010 Chile signed the OECD Convention, becoming the first South American country to join the OECD (OECD.org). The economy started to show signs of a rebound in the fourth quarter of 2009, and GDP grew more than 5% in 2010 according to World Bank data. Chile achieved this growth despite the magnitude 8.8 earthquake that struck Chile in February 2010, which was one of the top ten strongest earthquakes on record (World Economic Forum Report). The earthquake and subsequent tsunamis it generated caused considerable damage near the epicenter, located about 70 miles from Concepcion—and about 200 miles southwest of Santiago. The Chilean Ministry of Finance estimated the total immediate losses were close to 17% of GDP (World Economic Forum Report 2013).

President Michelle Bachelet introduced tax reforms in 2014 trying to fight inequality and to provide access to education and health care. The reforms generate additional tax revenues equal to 3% of Chile's GDP, mostly by increasing corporate tax rates to OECD averages (World Economic Forum Report 2019).

5.2.2 Peru

When Ollanta Humala was elected president of Peru in 2011, inequality was the biggest challenge for his administration (COFACE economic study). Poor infrastructure has always hindered the spread of growth to Peru's non-coastal areas. The Humala administration passed several economic stimulus packages in 2014 to bolster growth (World Economic Forum Report 2016). These reforms include reforms to environmental regulations in order to spur investment in Peru's lucrative mining sector. This move was opposed by some environmental groups. But in 2015, mining investment fell as global commodity prices remained low and social conflicts plagued the sector.

Peru continued its free trade policy under the Humala administration. Peru has signed trade deals with the US, Canada, Singapore, China, Korea, Mexico, Japan, the EU, the European Free Trade Association, Chile, Thailand, Costa Rica, Panama, Venezuela, Honduras, concluded negotiations with Guatemala and the Trans-Pacific Partnership, and begun trade talks with El Salvador, India, and Turkey (WTO). Peru also has signed a trade pact with Chile, Colombia, and Mexico, called the Pacific Alliance, that seeks integration of services, capital, investment and movement of people (USSTR.gov). Since the US–PTPA entered into force in total trade between Peru and the United States has doubled (World Economic Forum Report 2013).

President Pedro Pablo Kuczynski succeeded Humala in July 2016 (BBC). Kuczynski has been focusing on economic reforms and free-market policies aimed at boosting investment in Peru. Mining output increased significantly in 2016–2017 and that helped Peru attain one of the highest GDP growth rates in Latin America (World Economic Forum Report 2017). Economic performance was depressed by delays in infrastructure mega-projects and the start of a corruption scandal associated with a Brazilian firm (BBC). If corruption is kept under control there is no reason why Peru should maintain strong growth in 2019

5.3 Political Risk

5.3.1 Chile

According to the World Bank data Chile had an average growth rate of 1.7% through 2014–2017. In 2018, GDP saw a sharp rise. The stronger performance was mainly because of relatively higher copper prices and the rebound in business confidence. The reason for higher business confidence can be attributed to the election of the business-friendly President Sebastián Piñera (World Economic Forum Report 2017). These factors also contributed to a rebound in investments after four consecutive years of economic slowdown. A low inflation level and an accommodative monetary policy have also contributed to boosting household consumption.

In 2019, investments should remain robust. But in 2019 household consumption could observe some deceleration. This can happen due to the side effects of inflation moving back to the 3% target (COFACE).

It was driven by a low comparison base and by recent exchange rate depreciation and the central bank is implementing a tightening monetary cycle (COFACE). In 2019, the employment figures were less than impressive in light of a growing labor force (World Bank data). Downside risk to the activity outlook comes mainly from an escalation of the US–China trade war, which could hurt global growth as well as copper prices. China and the United States represent the main destinations of Chile's exports, representing 28% and 14%, respectively, of total exports in 2017 (Export.gov). Additionally, copper accounts for 10% of the country's GDP, 25% of its fiscal revenues, and 50% of its export earnings (World Bank data).

According to the World Bank data the current account deficit widened in 2018. The relatively weaker outcome is primarily because of the trade balance. as imports were driven by higher energy prices, the rise of import faster than exports. As copper prices lost momentum along the year due to the global trade protectionist rhetoric.

Copper and energy prices should remain at similar levels in 2019 (COFACE), no big changes in balance are expected. Despite the relatively higher current account deficit, foreign direct investments in Chile are enough to ensure the external balance. The country holds foreign exchange reserves worth roughly 14% of GDP, or seven months of import coverage, in addition to sovereign wealth funds estimated at around 9% of GDP (World Bank data).

Chile is not totally immune to shifts in foreign investors' mood toward emerging economies. The country holds an external debt of 60% of its GDP, over 70% of which is owed by the private sector—21% banks and financial institutions, 79% non-financial institutions (COFACE). In late 2018, Congress approved a general banking law to move toward the Basel III standard (BBC). Regarding the fiscal balance, the robust initial position of the public finances has helped mitigate the negative impact of sluggish activity in 2014–2017. In the wake of rebounding activity, the government was able to reduce the fiscal deficit in 2018. In 2019, fiscal consolidation is expected to gain further momentum, in line with the goal of reducing the structural deficit by 0.2 percentage point per year, until reaching a deficit of 1% in 2022 (COFACE).

The incumbent President Sebastián Piñera from the center-right Chile Vamos alliance took office in March 2018 (BBC). His party or the main opposition holds a congressional majority, so it would be impossible to build consensus to pass reforms, and he will struggle to find support among the opposition for measures such as reducing labor unions' strength and mining regulations.

Chile holds a highly privatized pension system that was introduced in the 1980s under the Pinochet dictatorship (Enero-Febrero 2003). Over the years, the combination of an aging population, insufficient pension contribution rates, poor-paying jobs, and high unemployment rates have contributed to low payouts. Although the proposal goes in direction of the opposition in some areas, the government might need to make some adjustments to the initial proposal in order to pass the bill through Congress.

5.3.2 Peru

According to World Bank data, GDP reported a bright improvement in 2018, after 2017 marked by strong floods triggered by El Niño and by the suspension of public investment due to corruption scandals. Activity growth was also spurred by robust domestic demand. Investments rebounded, both private and public, backed by a stronger political environment. In addition, household consumption also gained strength on the back of a controlled inflation and accommodative monetary policy.

According to the forecast of COFACE Peru should observe a similar rate of growth in 2019. Terms of trade should stay close to the levels of 2018, supporting exports and investments in the sector. In 2019, according to COFACE forecast household consumption is expected to remain strong due to favorable inflation and monetary policy.

There are some downside risks related to the external scenario in Peru. An escalation in the trade dispute between the United States and China can have a major impact as China and United States are the major trading partner of Peru (export.gov). A stronger tightening in US monetary policy can also have some impact on the trade between United States and Peru. While there are some new domestic political tensions, a possible further escalation, should not cause strong impact in economic activity, as there is a broad consensus on pro-business policies in Peru.

Most Latin American currencies depreciated in 2018 due to a shift in investors' mood toward emerging markets (World Economic Forum Report 2018). But the novo sol (the currency of Peru) has remained broadly stable because of Peru's sound external position compared to other economies (IMF Report). In the past two years, Peru has registered low deficits in its current account, driven by stronger trade surpluses due to improvements in terms of trade (World Bank data). In addition, the low external imbalance has been comfortably sheltered by FDI. Moreover, the country's international foreign exchange reserves are among the highest in the region relative to GDP, at 29.5% as of the end of 2017 (World Bank data). The dollarization of the banking system has fallen over the last decade to 29% of credit and 32% of deposits at July 2018 from 51% and 46%, respectively, at December 2008 (COFACE).

Kuczynski's resignation was triggered by evidence of corruption with the Brazilian construction group Odebrecht (BBC). A new escalation of political tensions is possible. In September 2018, the Attorney General reopened a corruption investigation into the failed contract of an airport, which had led Mr Vizcarra to resign as Transport Minister in May 2017 (*The Guardian*). In October 2018, Keiko Fujimori, leader of Fuerza Popular—opposition party with a large majority in Congress, was detained over allegations of illicit campaign contributions (*The Guardian*). All this corruption in politics keeps on imposing addition political risk on Peru that is preventing Peru from achieving its potential economic success.

5.4 Types of Legal Systems Existing in Chile and Peru

5.4.1 *Chile*

Chile's founders drew on the example of the United States in designing the institutions of government, they drew on Roman law and Spanish and French traditions, particularly the Napoleonic Code, in designing the country's judicial system (Burr 1967).

The 1925 constitution introduced reforms aimed at improving the judicial system by guaranteeing judicial independence. Chile's justice system established itself as one of the best on the South American continent, despite a serious lack of resources and inadequate attention to the needs of the nation's poorest citizens (Haas 2008).

During the Popular Unity government, the Supreme Court repeatedly clashed with the president and his associates. The Allende government viewed the court as a conservative and inflexible power, obsessed with a literal definition of a law designed to protect the privileges of private property against the new logic of a revolutionary time. The Supreme Court retorted vehemently that its task was simply to follow the dictates of the law, not to change it to suit some other objective.

The courts had much less difficulty dealing with the military regime, which left the court system virtually unbroken. As soon as the courts accepted the legitimacy of the military junta as the new executive and legislative power, they worked diligently to adjudicate matters in conformity with the new decree laws, even when the latter violated the spirit and letter of the constitution. In particular, the courts did nothing to address the serious issue of human rights violations, continuously deferring to the military and security services. The Supreme Court saw its own jurisdiction severely eroded as the military justice system expanded to encompass a wide range of national security matters that went far beyond institutional concerns.

According to the 1925 constitution, modified somewhat by the 1980 document, the Supreme Court can declare a particular law, decree law, or international treaty "inapplicable because of unconstitutionality". This does not invalidate the statute or measure for all cases, only for the one under consideration. Another important function of the Supreme Court is the administration of the court system. The organization and jurisdiction of Chile's courts were established in the Organic Code of the Tribunals (Law 7241) adopted in 1943. This law was modified on several occasions; two recent instances are the organic constitutional Law 18,969 of March 10, 1990, and Law 19,124 of February 2, 1992. Chile's ordinary courts consist of the Supreme Court, the appellate courts (*cortes de apelación*), major claims courts, and various local courts (*juzgados de letras*). There is also a series of special courts, such as the juvenile courts, labor courts, and military courts in time of peace. The local courts consist of one or more tribunals specifically assigned to each of the country's communes, Chile's smallest administrative units. In larger jurisdictions, the local courts may specialize in criminal cases or civil cases, as defined by law.

Chile has sixteen appellate courts, each with jurisdiction over one or more provinces. The majority of the courts have four members, although the two largest courts have thirteen members, and Santiago's Appellate Court (Corte de Apelación) has twenty-five. The Supreme Court consists of seventeen members, who select a president from their number for a three-year term. The Supreme Court carries out its functions with separate chambers consisting of at least five judges each, presided over by the most senior member or the president of the court.

Members and prosecutors of the Supreme Court are appointed by the president of the republic, who selects them from a slate of five persons proposed by the court itself. At least two must be senior judges on an appellate court. The others can include candidates from outside the judicial system.

The justices and prosecutors of each appellate court are also appointed by the president from a slate of three candidates submitted by the Supreme Court, only one of whom can be from outside the judicial system. In order to be appointed, ordinary judges at the local level are appointed by the president from a slate of three persons submitted by a court of appeals. They must be lawyers, must be at least twenty-five years old, and must have judicial experience. Ministers of the appeals courts must be at least thirty-two years old, and Supreme Court ministers must be at least thirty-six years old, with a specified number of years of judicial or legal experience. Judges serve for life and cannot be removed except for inappropriate behavior.

The relationship between the Aylwin administration and the Supreme Court was tense. Pinochet offered extraordinary retirement bonuses to the eldest court members to ensure the appointment of relatively young judges who were friends of the outgoing regime. The parties of the CPD were highly critical of these appointments and made no secret of their strong disapproval of the Supreme Court's behavior under the military government, particularly its complete disregard for the massive violations of human rights. Responding to these concerns, the Aylwin administration introduced constitutional reform legislation that would overhaul the nomination procedure for Supreme Court ministers, create a separate administrative structure for the judicial branch, and obligate the Supreme Court to take a more vigilant role in the protection of human rights. These reform efforts failed because the parties of the right refused to go along with the change in the face of strong opposition from the Supreme Court, which was fearful that it would lose its prerogatives and concerned that the judicial system would become "politicized". Still pending as Aylwin's term neared its end were reforms of the military justice system with its authority to try civilians in areas of national security and to judge military personnel even when charged with a criminal or civil crime against civilians.

5.4.2 *Peru*

The Supreme Court of Justice was the highest judicial authority in the nation. The twelve Supreme Court justices were nominated by the president and served for life. The nominations had to be approved by the Senate. The Supreme Court of Justice was also responsible for drawing up the budget for the judiciary, which was then submitted to the executive. The budget could be no less than 2% of the government's expenditures. Under the Supreme Court of Justice were the Superior Courts, which were seated in the capitals of judicial districts; the Courts of First Instance, which sat in provincial capitals and were divided into civil, criminal, and special branches; and the justices of the peace in all local centers.

Several other judicial functions are worthy of note. The public prosecutor's office was appointed by the president and was responsible for overseeing the independence of judges and the administration of justice, representing the community at trials, and defending people before the public administration. Public attorneys, who are also appointed by the president, defend the interests of the state. The office of the Public Ministry was made up of the attorney general and attorneys before the Supreme Court of Justice, Superior Courts, and the Courts of First Instance. Public attorneys defended the rights of citizens in the public interest against encroachment by public officials.

The National Elections Board established voting laws, registered parties and their candidates, and supervised elections. It also had the power to void elections if the electoral procedures were invalid. The six-member board was composed of one person elected by the Supreme Court of Justice, one by the Bar of Lima, one by the law faculty deans of the national universities, and three Peru's regional boards.

Although in theory the judicial system was independent and guaranteed at least minimal operating financial support, in practice this was far from the case. The system had been hampered by scarce resources, a tradition of executive manipulation, and inadequate protection of officials in the face of threats from insurgents and drug traffickers. Even without the existence of guerrilla movements, the system was inadequately staffed to deal with the number of cases from criminal violations. It was not uncommon for detainees to spend several years in prison awaiting a hearing. In addition, in the emergency zones, where guerrillas were operating, security forces have had virtual carte blanche in the areas of interrogation and detention, and suspects often have been held incommunicado. Imprisoned suspects awaiting trial have subsisted in medieval conditions

The executive branch traditionally manipulated the judiciary for its own purposes, using its ability to appoint and remove certain judges for its own political ends. For example, when a Superior Court judge ruled that President García's nationalization of Peru's banks was unconstitutional, García merely replaced him with a judge from his party, the American Popular Revolutionary Alliance, who then ruled in his favor (Van Klaveren 1996).

It also was common for known terrorists or drug traffickers to be released for "insufficient evidence" by judges with no protection whatsoever but with responsibility for trying those suspected of terrorism. Largely because of corruption or inefficiency in the system, only 5% of those detained for terrorism had been sentenced by 1991. Those responsible for administering justice were under threat from all sides of the political spectrum: guerrilla movements, drug traffickers, and military-linked paramilitary squads (Van Klaveren 1996).

5.5 Contracts and Agreements: How Are They Documented?

5.5.1 *Chile*

Most companies tend to be very hierarchical, and people expect to work within clearly established lines of authority. Decision makers are usually top executives who will consider the best interest of the group or organization. In most cases, they will consult with others to reach greater consensus and support. They rarely delegate their authority, so it is important to deal with senior executives. Gaining access to top managers can be difficult. Subordinates could strongly influence the final decision. Maintaining good relationships with these intermediaries is crucial to be successful in Chile. Decision-making can be a slow process that requires much patience. Attempts to rush or put pressure on the process are not likely to succeed. When making decisions, businesspeople may not rely much on rules or laws. They usually consider the specific situation rather than applying universal principles. Personal feelings and experiences weigh more strongly than empirical evidence and other objective facts do. Chileans are often uneasy with change and reluctant to take risks (export.gov).

Capturing and exchanging written understandings after meetings and at key negotiation stages is useful since oral statements and even handshakes are not always dependable. Relying on interim agreements is not the norm, even if they come in the form of written protocols. Any part of an agreement may still change significantly before both parties sign the final contract. Written contracts tend to be lengthy and often spell out detailed terms and conditions for the core agreements as well as for many eventualities. Writing up and signing the contract is a formality. Chileans believe that the primary strength of an agreement lies in the partners' commitment rather than in its written documentation. It is strongly advisable to consult a local legal expert before signing a contract.

Contracts are usually dependable, and the agreed terms are viewed as binding. Although partners are expected to remain somewhat flexible, requests to change contract details after signature may meet with strong resistance.

5.5.2 *Peru*

Corruption and bribery are quite common in Peru's public and private sectors. People may draw the line differently, viewing minor payments as rewards for getting a job done rather than as bribes. There is a fine line between giving gifts and bribing. What one may consider a bribe, a Peruvian may view as only a nice gift (export.gov).

Capturing and exchanging written understandings after meetings and at key negotiation stages is useful. Oral commitments may sound stronger than what Peruvian counterparts may be willing to put in writing. Interim agreements are not final, even if they come in the form of written protocols. Any part of an agreement may still change significantly before both parties sign the final contract. Written contracts tend to be lengthy and often spell out detailed terms and conditions for the core agreements as well as for many eventualities. Writing up and signing the contract is a formality. Peruvians believe that the primary strength of an agreement lies in the partners' commitment rather than in its written documentation. Signed contracts may not always be honored. This depends to no small degree on the strength of the continuing relationship between the contract partners. Staying in touch and maintaining the trust Peruvian business partner is trivial. Business partners usually expect the other side to remain flexible if conditions change, which may include agreeing to modify contract terms. Given the relatively unstable political and economic situation in the country a potential investor needs to keep an open eye in going into a business contract.

5.6 Obstacles to Entrepreneurship

5.6.1 *Chile*

Chile is the best evaluated economy in Latin America and one of the best evaluated among emerging economies worldwide because of sustained economic growth and social progress, coupled with governmental changes designed to attract foreign direct investment (World Economic Forum

Report 2019). The country has remarkable fiscal discipline which has underlined GDP growth of 4.8% between 2004 and 2011 (World Bank data).

FDI plays a central role in Chile's economic growth and development, and there has been a sustained increase in levels of overseas investment in recent years. This has helped to enhance Chile's competitiveness by contributing not only resources and new markets but also technological development, specialized know-how, and inputs conducive to innovation and entrepreneurship.

The World Bank and International Finance Corporation (IFC) rank Chile 32nd in the world for ease of starting a business. There are seven procedures to complete when first starting up and a long line of bureaucratic challenges. That includes notarized articles of incorporation, a registration certificate, a tax registration number, and a "patente municipal" working license, as well as registering with the appropriate authorities.

Based on the World Bank doing business report, obtaining construction permits is a lengthy procedure in Chile largely because of the number of steps it takes to receive them. Businesses must navigate their way through 15 requirements and many stages are carried out by disparate governing bodies and firms. Obtaining indication on water and sewage availability, for example, must be completed with a sanitation company, and checks with the telecom company, the environmental health services, SERVIU and DOM must all be conducted during the process.

Based on the World Bank doing business report, businesses will likely engage with La Compañía Chilena de Electricidad (CHILECTRA) when getting electricity, with documentation sent to the firm before an external inspection is carried out and the connection is made. Businesses are also required to receive approval of the internal installation works by the "Superintendencia de Electricidad y Combustibles (SEC)" before they receive final connection and a meter.

Based on the World Bank doing business report, registering property is a similarly laborious process, although it takes far less time than elsewhere in Latin America and the Caribbean. Businesses must request copies of property titles for the past 10 years, the "Certificado de Vigencia" and certificate of encumbrance from the registry in order to register a property, and also need to pay land tax, sign the public deed, and obtain a Property Certificate and a Mortgages and Ownership Limitations Certificate.

Based on the World Bank business report, getting credit is quite difficult in Chile, despite its robust financial sector. Protecting investors is similarly concerning, although it performs far better than its South American and Caribbean counterparts.

Based on the World Bank doing business report, there are six tax payments to make each year in Chile, but each step can be a painstaking procedure. Employment taxes, for example, take 124 hours of the company's time, and value-added tax (VAT) takes the same amount. Cross border trade is a relatively cheap endeavor in Chile, but it can take a long time to complete. There are 15 steps involved in exporting goods and 12 when importing. Enforcing contracts takes significantly fewer days than in the rest of Latin America, but takes a similar amount of procedures. The judicial system efficiently processes the claim, but filing and service adds a large amount of time to the overall procedure.

Based on the World Bank doing business report, resolving insolvency takes an average of 3.2 years in Chile, which is longer than both the OECD average and the Latin America and Caribbean average. The recovery rates are also rather low, dropping under both regional averages.

Based on the World Bank doing business report, establishing trust and connecting as people is fundamental to successful business relationships in Chile, and initial visits should always be used to build a rapport and show who you are. Unlike some nations, the relationship takes precedent over business matters, to begin with, and companies should be aware of cultural quirks before leaving for the country.

5.6.2 *Peru*

Peru has one of the fastest growing economies in Latin America, even taking into account the slower 2017 growth of 2.5%—below that of 2016 (3.9%) and 2015 (3.26%) and below 2.8% which is the official estimate given by the Ministry of Economy and Finance (World Bank data). However, for 2019, according to IMF projections, the growth should be 4%. Economic growth has been driven by an increase in private investment, modernization, and development.

Peru offers a favorable, if complicated, legal framework for foreign investment and a friendly investment environment, reflected in the World Bank Ease of Doing Business Survey, where Peru ranks 58th overall. The top industries in Peru include mining, manufacturing, energy, petrochemical, tourism, and real estate.

Based on the World Bank doing business report, starting a business in Peru, is a bureaucratic process, ranking it 114th in the World Bank Ease of

Doing Business Survey. It takes around 27 days and seven procedures to set up a business. The heaviest procedures are signing the deed of incorporation before a notary public and filing it online with the Public Registry of Commerce, which takes 8 days, and obtaining a Municipal license from the District Council which takes 15 days. When the shareholders are from abroad, the incorporation process usually takes much more time.

Based on the World Bank doing business report, companies looking to do business and hire workers in Peru must be aware of all the local payroll rules and how to remain compliant to the payroll cycles. Peru's Compensation for Length of Service (CTS) is a legal benefit given to workers for their time spent working for a company, made at the time of retirement. The CTS is deposited biannually in the worker's bank of choice. Employers deposit 50% in May, for the period worked from November to April, and 50% in November for the period worked from May to October. If a company does not submit CTS payment in a timely manner it will be required to pay interest, accrued from the due date until the date the payment is made.

The World Bank ranks Peru 61st for ease of dealing with construction permits and 44th for registering a property. Dealing with construction permits takes 15 procedures and an astonishing 188 days! Other registrations include obtaining a construction license from the Municipality (licencia de obra para edificación nueva), which takes 45 days and obtaining drinking water service installation, which takes 50 days.

Based on the World Bank doing business report, registering a property is much more straightforward with just five procedures and takes 8 days. Obtaining electricity in Peru takes a couple of months and involves submitting an application to Luz del Sur and awaiting feasibility study and budget, which takes 17 days. This is followed by signing the supply contract and awaiting completion of external works by Luz del Sur, which can take around 50 days.

Based on the World Bank doing business report, transfer Pricing obligations in Peru are now being regulated in more detail than ever before. This could mean that intra-group operations will be subjected to greater scrutiny by the Peruvian tax authorities. The changes include more detail required for all files, including the minimum information required, such as identifying the personnel on whom the company's management and administration depend. Having local support is essential.

Based on the World Bank doing business report, maintaining open, honest and compliant business practices is important in a country where corruption is still a big issue. There was an infamous case last year, involving a large Brazilian construction company, which admitted paying bribes in more than half the countries in Latin America, including Peru. This not only prompted a change in legislation, but also had a major impact on the local economy. Peruvian legislation now recognizes the corporate criminal liability applicable to bribes, so companies need to maintain legal, transparent business practices which are fully compliant with the law.

Based on the World Bank doing business report, court rulings and the degree of enforcement are often inconsistent and allegations of political corruption and outside interference in the judicial system are common. While the legal framework for the protection of intellectual property (IP) in Peru has improved over the past ten years, unfortunately enforcement remains weak. Stricter penalties for IP theft have been brought into law, yet they have still to be implemented. There have also yet to be convictions and penalties for IP violations.

The World Bank Ease of Doing Business Survey ranks Peru 121st for paying taxes. It involves nine payments per year and 260 hours. Profit and labor taxes are the main ones, with corporate tax at 29.5%. All residents are taxed on income that they earn worldwide, while non-residents are taxed only on Peruvian earned income. For the purposes of taxation, a resident is a Peruvian national or a foreign national that has spent more than 183 days a year in the country.

VAT is added to most goods for sale, particularly imported items and some services. The rate is 18% and this can make the cost of some imported items seem quite high. In light of this, locally produced goods provide value for money. Stamp duty is not payable in Peru on property purchases.

Based on the World Bank doing business report, Peru is a little challenging and bureaucratic regarding contracts and insolvency. When enforcing contracts, anticipate around 430 days, 175 of which is enforcing the court judgment. This can cost around 36% of the claim. Dispute settlement generally remains problematic in Peru, and therefore it is recommended to include an arbitration clause in commercial agreements. Resolving insolvency takes over 3 years and the recovery rate is only 30 cents on the dollar.

Based on the World Bank doing business report, some of the cultural considerations you may need to factor in when doing business in Peru include handshakes as the most common greeting when being introduced. While shaking with the right hand, it is common practice to touch the arm of the other person with your left hand, especially among men. Or, when introducing a male and female, it is common practice for them to kiss each other once on the cheek. This practice is common among urban people, but not among Andean people who prefer handshaking and a hug. In conversations, relationships can be affected by volume and tone of voice: Peruvians usually speak softly, as speaking loudly is considered disrespectful.

5.7 Discussion

5.7.1 Chile

Chile is a success story in the Asia Pacific. The democratic government assumed after the military regime imposed a cluster of political and economic institutions enshrined in the Political Constitution of 1980. It included a high level of military entitlements, but also neoliberal rules aiming at consolidating the neoliberal policies and institutions regarding the economic and social policies that had been implemented during the 80s by the Pinochet regime (Robeldo 2013). Confronted with the requirements of avoiding an authoritarian regression, and with the need of reaching a basic level of democratic governance after the deep breakdown of 1973, the legacy of a prolonged authoritarian regime, as well as with the failure of the Import Substitution Industrialization (ISI) model, the democratic governments decided to maintain some policies of economic liberalization and fiscal responsiveness, but to apply a growing set of social policies to address the very high social cost after several years of IMF's structural adjustment policies (Robeldo 2013).

One of the features of the Chilean democratic experience has been the centrality of its foreign policy and international economic insertion for its economic performance. After 1990, Chile decided to maintain the process of economic liberalization and internationalization that has been initiated by the military government because of its importance for the growth of a small-scale economy. Other important political consequence of the Chilean Open Regionalism was the limits this option imposed regarding its relationship with Brazil and MERCOSUR. Despite its natural regional priorities, the Chilean Administration assessed that the country was not in a condition to return to higher tariffs, so it could not enter MERCOSUR as a full member. Chile understood that Brazil and other countries of the Southern American block had a legitimate interest in protecting their industries. Chile was interested in participating in "new regionalism" because of political, strategic and even economic considerations. Chile entered MERCOSUR as an associated state, signing a Treaty of Association in 1996, which included a bilateral FTA (Britannica).

The Chilean economy became also more regionally diversified, thus also less dependent on changes in the international economy, and more resilient. Politically, it means a higher degree of political autonomy. While in 1990 52% for the exports were sent to Europe, 21% to Asia, 15% to the NAFTA, 10% to Latin America, the 2% to the rest of the World, in 2009 45% of the exports were led to Asia, 20% to the EU, 18% to Latin America, 16% to the NAFTA, and 1% to other countries. Trade agreements also regulate non-tariffs areas, like services, investments, intellectual property, competitiveness, environment, and labor standards for the private and public sectors, increasing the institutional dimension of its economic competitiveness (Robeldo 2013). This had a positive impact for Foreign Direct Investment (FDI), which became 62% of the GDP in 2012, when Chile received a record of US$ 26 billions of FDI, the second in the region after Brazil (Heine 2013).

5.7.2 Peru

Since the start of the twenty-first century, Peru has experienced consistent economic growth, poverty reduction, and democratic advancement. The US–Peru Trade Promotion Agreement (PTPA) entered into force on February 1, 2009, increasing incentives for economic and social cooperation between the two countries (USTR.gov). President Martin Vizcarra assumed office in March 2018 after President Pedro Pablo Kuczynksi resigned over corruption allegations (BBC). President Vizcarra announced a platform for improving governance, combatting corruption, and improving the lives of Peruvians through investments in infrastructure and social services. Peru has experienced impressive economic growth rates and low inflation, but challenges remain. For example, despite a dramatic drop in poverty levels, wide disparities in income and access to basic services remain. Corruption remains endemic at all levels of government, and transnational criminal organizations have expanded beyond narcotics trafficking into trafficking in illegally mined gold, timber, counterfeit currency, and wildlife.

5.8 Conclusion

5.8.1 *Chile*

The current President Sebastián Piñera from the center-right Chile Vamos alliance took office in March 2018 (Forbes 2018). Mr Piñera was elected with his pledges to reduce mining regulations, to make adjustments to President Michelle Bachelet's labor reform, to simplify tax rules, to reduce some corporate taxes, and to narrow the fiscal deficit. Unfortunately, neither his party nor the main opposition holds a congressional majority, and he will struggle to find support among the opposition for measures such as reducing labor unions' strength and mining regulations.

In June 2018, Mr Piñera announced that he would not cut the corporate tax rate that Bachelet's government raised to 27% (Forbes 2018). His rationale of backtracking his campaign promise is that the rate would help solve the fiscal imbalance and fund social reforms needed for the education, health, and pension systems. Subsequently, at the end of October 2018, Mr Piñera presented a pension reform. The country holds a highly-privatized pension system that was introduced in the 1980s under the Pinochet dictatorship. Over the years, the combination of an aging population, insufficient pension contribution rates, poor-paying jobs, and high unemployment rates have contributed to low payouts. Although the proposal goes in direction of the opposition in some areas, the government might need to make some adjustments to the initial proposal in order to pass the bill through Congress. If the political stability is ensured, Chile has a very bright future ahead.

5.8.2 *Peru*

President Pedro Pablo Kuczynski (PPK) of the center-right Peruvians for Change party resigned in March 2018 (Britannica). Pablo Kuczynski faced two impeachments vote in three months. Pablo Kuczynski's resignation was prompted by evidence of corruption with the Brazilian construction group Odebrecht (BBC).

First Vice-President Martín Vizcarra took office (Britannica). Responding to the widespread anger due to the corruption scandals, Martín Vizcarra took a harder line with the opposition-run Congress. Martín Vizcarra has threatened to invoke a constitutional procedure to dissolve the house if it fails to grant him a vote of confidence to advance with four constitutional reforms to combat graft. In October 2018, the Congress approved the legislation, representing a victory to the government. A referendum on the reforms was held on December 9 (*The Guardian*).

However, a new escalation of political tensions is possible: in September 2018, the Attorney General reopened a corruption investigation into the failed contract of an airport, which had led Mr Vizcarra to resign as Transport Minister in May 2017. Moreover, in October 2018, Keiko Fujimori, leader of Fuerza Popular (opposition party with a large majority in Congress), was detained over allegations of illicit campaign contributions. In addition, while Ms Fujimori's popularity has declined in recent months due to the scandals, her party is likely to continue using its power in Congress to oppose President Vizcarra (*The Guardian*). Peru has tremendous potential. But corruption and political instability is the only thing that is holding Peru back. If good sense prevails and Peru can live without corrupt politicians, the sky is the limit for Peru and it will be a dream destination for investors.

References

Burr, Robert. 1967. *By Reason or Force: Chile and the Balancing of Power in South America, 1830–1905.* Berkeley: University of California Press.

Clinton, Hillary. 2011. America's Pacific Century. *Foreign Policy*, 189 (October 11): 56–63.

Enero-Febrero. 2003. *The Changing Nature of Asia-Latin American Relations*, ed. German King, José Carlos Mattos, Nanno Mulder, and Osvaldo Rosales, 2013. Santiago: ECLAC.

Haas, Richard. 2008. The Age of Nonpolarity: What Will Follow U.S. Dominance. *Foreign Affairs*, 87 (3, May/June): 44–56.

Heine, Jorge. 2013. *Nuevo Orden Internacional y Política Exterior de Chile*. Unpublished Paper.

http://data.imf.org/. Accessed Multiple Times Latest on May 12, 2019.

https://data.worldbank.org. Accessed Multiple Times Latest on May 12, 2019.

https://www.coface.com/Economic-Studies-and-Country-Risks/Chile. Accessed May 11, 2019.

https://www.coface.com/Economic-Studies-and-Country-Risks/Peru. Accessed May 11, 2019.

https://en.portal.santandertrade.com/establish-overseas/chile/foreign-investment. Accessed May 11, 2019.

https://en.portal.santandertrade.com/establish-overseas/peru/investing. Accessed March 14, 2019.

http://www.gob.cl/2015/10/13/discurso-de-la-presidenta-de-la-republica-al-anunciar-el-proceso-constituyente/. Accessed March 14, 2019.

http://www.gob.cl/2015/10/13/infografia-conoce-las-etapas-del-proceso-constituyente/. Accessed March 14, 2019.
https://www.unaconstitucionparachile.cl/. Accessed March 14, 2019.
http://www.gob.cl/conoce-se-construyeron-las-bases-ciudadanas-del-proceso-constituyente/. Accessed March 14, 2019.
http://www.comision-pensiones.cl/. Accessed March 14, 2019.
http://www.duna.cl/media/2017/11/INFORME-FINAL-Candidaturas-Chile-20NOV-.pdf. Accessed March 14, 2019.
https://www.forbes.com/sites/noahkirsch/2017/12/18/this-billionaire-just-became-president-of-chile/#578b29f45899. Accessed March 14, 2019.
https://www.britannica.com/biography/Pedro-Pablo-Kuczynski. Accessed March 14, 2019.
https://www.theguardian.com/world/2018/mar/23/martin-vizcarra-peru-president-kuczynski. Accessed March 14, 2019.
https://www.bbc.com/news/business-39194395. Accessed March 14, 2019.
https://ustr.gov/trade-agreements/free-trade-agreements/chile-fta. Accessed March 14, 2019.
https://www.wto.org/english/thewto_e/countries_e/chile_e.htm. Accessed March 14, 2019.
https://www.oecd.org/about/members-and-partners/. Accessed March 14, 2019.
https://www.worldatlas.com/articles/the-richest-countries-in-south-america.html. Accessed April 12, 2019.
https://www.worldatlas.com/articles/the-world-s-leading-silver-producing-countries.html. Accessed March 14, 2019.
http://www3.weforum.org/docs/GCR2016–2017/05FullReport/TheGlobalCompetitivenessReport2016-2017_FINAL.pdf. Accessed April 2, 2019.
http://www3.weforum.org/docs/GCR2017–2018/05FullReport/TheGlobalCompetitivenessReport2017%E2%80%932018.pdf. Accessed April 2, 2019.
https://www.export.gov. Accessed April 2, 2019.
http://www.doingbusiness.org/en/reports/global-reports/doing-business-2019. Accessed May 11, 2019.
International Monetary Fund. 2013. World Economic Outlook Database. http://www.imf.org/external/pubs/ft/weo/2013/01/weodata/index.aspx. Accessed May 30, 2019.
Robeldo, Marcos. 2013. Chile and the Asia Pacific: Toward a New Foreign Policy Cycle. Wilson Center Latin American Center Policy Paper.
U.S. Geological Survey, Mineral Commodity Summaries, February 2019.

Van Klaveren, Alberto. 1996. Understanding Latin American Foreign Policies. In *Latin American Nations in World Politics*, 2nd ed., ed. Heraldo Muñoz and Joseph S. Tulchin. Boulder: Westview Press.
World Economic Forum, 2013. Global Competitiveness Report 2012–2013. http://reports.weforum.org/global-competitiveness-report-2012-2013/. Accessed April 2, 2019.

CHAPTER 6

The Economic Climate

6.1 Introduction

Economic Climate touches upon long-term economic condition prevailing in the economy and its predictable patterns of growth, decline, potential, and movement. The term explains how generally countries economic condition varies widely. This chapter sheds more light on the economic climate of Chile and Peru particularly monetary, fiscal, and commercial systems. Each subtopic will be discussed for better precision and consideration.

6.2 Background

6.2.1 Chile

Economy of Chile is market-oriented. The hallmark of Chile's economy is the large amount of foreign trade. Chile also has strong financial institutions. Chile has one of the strongest sovereign bond ratings in South America according to trending economics. In Table 6.1, Chile's most recent sovereign bond rating has been displayed. Moody rating for Chile is A1, S&P has rated Chile A+ and Fitch has rated Chile A. Exports of goods and services account for approximately one-third of GDP according to World Bank data, with commodities making up some 60% of total exports. Copper is Chile's top export and provides 20% of government revenue.

In early 1990s, Chile stood out as an economic reform role model. Since 1999, the GDP of Chile has averaged 4% per year. Chile expanded its

J. E. Spillan and M. N. Rahman, *Doing Business in Chile and Peru*,
https://doi.org/10.1007/978-3-030-25073-7_6

Table 6.1 Sovereign Bond rating of Chile

Agency	*Rating*	*Outlook*	*Date*
Moody's	A1	Stable	July 26, 2018
Moody's	Aa3	Negative	August 24, 2017
Fitch	A	Stable	August 11, 2017
S&P	A+	Stable	July 13, 2017

Source Sovereign credit ratings in Latin America and the Caribbean (ECLAC 2019)

established obligation to trade liberalization with the signing of a free trade agreement with the United States, which took effect on January 1, 2004.

Chile has a lot of bilateral or regional trade agreements. It has 57 agreements with the European Union, Mercosur, China, India, South Korea, and Mexico. Foreign direct investment inflows have increased to $15 billion in 2010, but FDI had dropped to about $7 billion in 2009 in the face of weakened investment throughout the world. Chile uses a countercyclical fiscal policy, storing surpluses in sovereign wealth funds during periods of high copper prices and economic growth, and allowing insufficiency spending only during periods of low copper prices and growth. In September 2008, that sovereign wealth totaled to more than $23 billion. Chile used $4 billion from this fund to finance a fiscal stimulus package to fend off recession.

In December 2009, the OECD requested Chile to become a full member, after a two-year period of compliance with organization mandates, and in May 2010 Chile signed the OECD Convention. Chile became the first South American country to join the OECD. The economy started to show signs of a recovery in the fourth quarter of 2009, and GDP grew more than 5% in 2010.

Chile achieved this growth despite the magnitude 8.8 earthquake that struck Chile in February 2010. The earthquake and consequent tsunamis caused extensive damage near the epicenter, located about 70 miles from Concepcion—and about 200 miles southwest of Santiago. The estimates the total immediate losses were close to 17% of GDP.

In 2014, tax reforms were introduced to fight inequality and to provide access to education and health care. The reforms are projected to generate additional tax revenues equal to 3% of Chile's GDP, mostly by increasing corporate tax rates to OECD averages.

Table 6.2 The richest countries in South America

Rank	*Country*	*Income (per capita)*
1	Chile	$24,588
2	Uruguay	$22,445
3	Argentina	$19,486
4	Brazil	$15,164
5	Colombia	$13,357
6	Suriname	$13,403
7	Peru	$12,994
8	Venezuela	$12,035
9	Ecuador	$9882
10	Paraguay	$9098
11	Guyana	$8173
12	Bolivia	$7174

Source WorldAtlas.com (2018)

Chile has the richest economy in South America in terms of per capita Income. The country covers an area of about 756,096.3 square km (291,930.4 square miles). According to worldometer in 2019 Chile has a population of 18,326,989. Chile is one of the most flourishing and steady economies of the continent and the World Bank ranks the Chilean economy as a high-income economy. Table 6.2 shows the ranking of per capita income of Latin American counties. It is the world's 30th most competitive country. Tables 6.3 and 6.4 show that Chile has constantly the second highest country among the South American countries in terms of per capita GDP and per capital GNI only slightly behind Uruguay. In 2017, Per Capita GNI of Chile was $13,610 only behind Uruguay's Per Capita GNI of $15,250. In 2017, Per Capita GDP of Chile was $15,346 only behind Uruguay's Per Capita GDP of $16246. The largest economic sectors by GDP in Chile are mining, business and personal services, wholesale, retail trade, and manufacturing.

Figure 6.1 shows that Chile's economic structure is mainly Agriculture based. 64% of GDP contribution comes from agriculture sector. Industrial sector contributes to 31% of GDP and the other 4% of GDP is contributed by service sector.

Figure 6.2 shows that Chile faced a recession in 2009, but since then recovered from the economic downturn very well. In 2010, 2011, and 2012 Chile enjoyed over 5% GDP growth rate. Since then the growth rate has slowed down but managed to avoid recession. Table 6.6 shows

Table 6.3 Per capita GDP of South American countries

Country name	*2013*	*2014*	*2015*	*2016*	*2017*
Chile	$15,941.40	$14,794.32	$13,736.64	$13,960.89	$15,346.45
Uruguay	$16,881.21	$16,737.90	$15,524.84	$15,298.35	$16,245.60
Argentina	$12,976.64	$12,245.26	$13,698.29	$12,654.35	$14,398.36
Brazil	$12,216.90	$12,026.62	$8750.22	$8650.38	$9812.28
Colombia	$8065.96	$7974.41	$6085.21	$5813.69	$6408.92
Suriname	$9491.57	$9554.56	$8617.76	$5645.33	$5317.39
Peru	$6583.12	$6492.05	$6053.11	$6031.37	$6571.93
Ecuador	$6074.09	$6396.63	$6150.16	$6099.32	$6273.49
Paraguay	$5967.66	$6146.66	$5447.12	$5360.99	$5823.77
Guyana	$3941.11	$4031.53	$4160.27	$4531.24	$4655.14
Bolivia	$2947.94	$3124.00	$3077.03	$3117.33	$3393.96

Source World Bank data (2019)

Table 6.4 Per capita GNI of South American countries

Country name	*2013*	*2014*	*2015*	*2016*	*2017*
Chile	$15,370.00	$15,120.00	$14,310.00	$13,590.00	$13,610.00
Uruguay	$15,580.00	$16,230.00	$15,830.00	$15,200.00	$15,250.00
Argentina	$12,770.00	$12,260.00	$12,510.00	$12,150.00	$13,030.00
Brazil	$12,730.00	$12,020.00	$10,090.00	$8860.00	$8610.00
Colombia	$7750.00	$8020.00	$7180.00	$6340.00	$5890.00
Suriname	$9020.00	$9340.00	$8770.00	$6660.00	$5150.00
Peru	$6250.00	$6340.00	$6160.00	$5950.00	$5960.00
Ecuador	$5830.00	$6130.00	$6000.00	$5840.00	$5920.00
Paraguay	$5550.00	$5840.00	$5670.00	$5430.00	$5470.00
Guyana	$3890.00	$4040.00	$4060.00	$4260.00	$4500.00
Bolivia	$2620.00	$2870.00	$3000.00	$3080.00	$3130.00

Source World Bank data (2019)

Chile produced 28% of world copper production being the highest copper producing country in the world.

6.2.2 *Peru*

Economy of Peru is dependent on its varied geography, that includes a dry lowland coastal region, the central high sierra of the Andes, and the dense forest of the Amazon. According to Worldometer population of Peru in

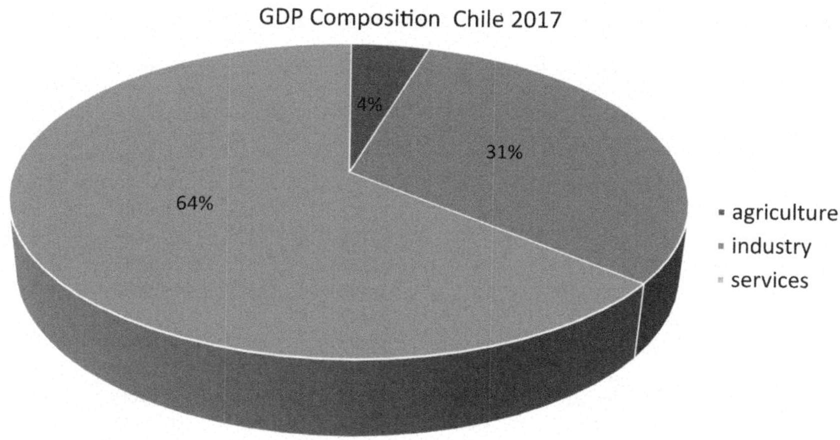

Fig. 6.1 Chile's GDP composition in 2017 (*Source* United Nations Statistics Division 2018)

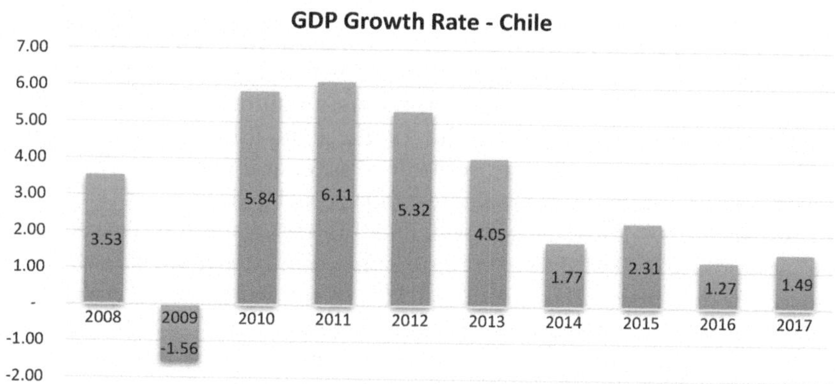

Fig. 6.2 The trend of Chile's GDP growth 2008–2017 (*Source* World Bank data 2019)

Table 6.5 The world's leading silver producing countries in 'tons

	Mine production				Reserves	
	2017	%	*2018*	%		%
United States	1030	4	900	3	25,000	4
Argentina	1020	4	1100	4	NA	NA
Australia	1200	4	1200	4	89,000	16
Bolivia	1240	5	1200	4	22,000	4
Chile	1260	5	1300	5	26,000	5
China	3500	13	3600	13	41,000	7
Mexico	6110	23	6100	23	37,000	7
Peru	4300	16	4300	16	110,000	20
Poland	1290	5	1300	5	110,000	20
Russia	1120	4	1200	4	45,000	8
Other countries	4770	18	4800	18	57,000	10
World total	26,840	100	27,000	100	562,000	100

Source US Geological Survey (2019)

2019 is 32.93 million. Peru covers a total area of 1,285,216 square kilometers (496,224 square miles). The economy is rich with a wide range of important mineral resources found in the mountainous and coastal areas. The coaster water of Peru has a lot of excellent fishing grounds. Peru has become the second largest producer of silver and copper in the world according to United States Geological Survey's (USGS) report published in February 2019. The data is provided in Tables 6.5 and 6.6. Peru's silver reserves stand at 110,000 tons, making it the country with the largest silver reserves in the world. Peru produced 16% of the world's total silver output in 2017 and 2018. Peru has 20% of world silver reserve. The deposits are enormous, and the country could quickly move up the rankings in the future.

Table 6.6 shows Peru produced 12% of world copper production being the second highest copper producing country in the world. The economy of Peru grew by an average of 5.6% per year from 2009 to 2013. During that time, the exchange rate was stable and inflation rate was low. This growth can be credited to high international prices for Peru's metals and minerals exports. The metals and minerals account for 55% of the country's total exports. Growth slipped from 2014 to 2017 as a result of weaker world prices metals and minerals.

Table 6.6 The world's leading copper producing countries in 'tons

	Mine production				Reserves	
	2017	%		%		%
United States	1260	6	1200	6	48,000	6
Australia	860	4	950	5	88,000	11
Chile	5500	28	5800	28	170,000	21
China	1710	9	1600	8	26,000	3
Congo	1090	.5	1200	6	20,000	2
Indonesia	622	3	780	4	51,000	6
Mexico	742	4	760	4	50,000	6
Peru	2450	12	2400	12	83,000	10
Russia	705	4	710	3	61,000	7
Zambia	794	4	870	4	19,000	2
Other countries	4250	21	4400	21	210,000	25
World total	19,983	100	20,670	100	826,000	100

Source US Geological Survey (2019)

Despite Peru's strong macroeconomic performance, dependence on minerals and metals exports and imported foodstuffs makes the economy exposed to international equilibrium price and exchange rate.

Rapid expansion in the economy of Peru combined with cash transfers and other programs have helped Peru to reduce the national poverty rate by over 35 percentage points since 2004. Inequality, however, persists and continued to be a challenge. Poor infrastructure hinders the spread of growth to Peru's non-coastal areas. In 2015, mining investment fell as global commodity prices remained low and social conflicts plagued the sector.

According to USTR data Peru's free trade policy continued since 2006, Peru has signed trade deals with the US, Canada, Singapore, China, Korea, Mexico, Japan, the EU, the European Free Trade Association, Chile, Thailand, Costa Rica, Panama, Venezuela, Honduras, concluded negotiations with Guatemala and the Trans-Pacific Partnership, and begun trade talks with El Salvador, India, and Turkey. Peru also has signed a trade pact with Chile, Colombia, and Mexico, called the Pacific Alliance, that seeks integration of services, capital, investment and movement of people. Since the US–Peru Trade Promotion Agreement entered into force in February 2009, total trade between Peru and the United States has doubled.

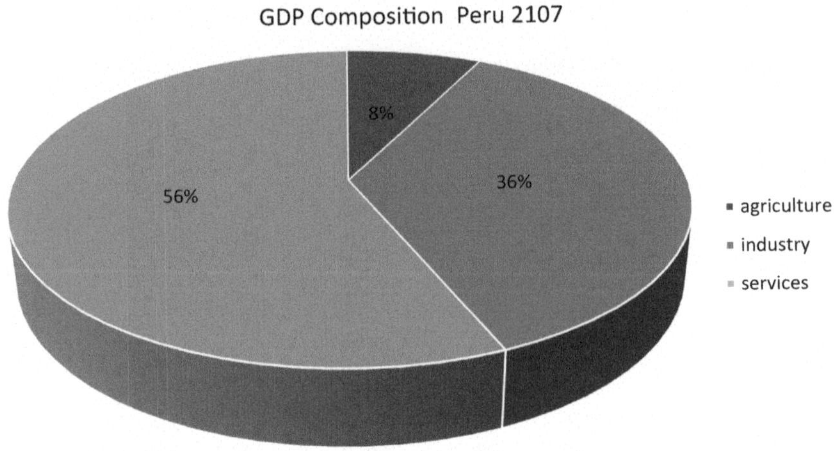

Fig. 6.3 Peru's GDP composition in 2017 (*Source* United Nations Statistics Division 2018)

Mining output increased significantly in 2016–2017 based on US Geological survey date, as a result Peru attained one of the highest GDP growth rates in Latin America. Unfortunately, economic performance was slowed down by delays in infrastructure megaprojects and the start of a corruption scandal associated with a Brazilian firm. Massive flooding in early 2017 also was a hampered growth.

Figure 6.3 shows that Peru's economic structure is mainly Agriculture based. 56% of GDP contribution comes from agriculture sector. Industrial sector contributes to 36% of GDP and the other 8% of GDP is contributed by service sector.

Figure 6.4 shows that Peru had impressive GDP growth rate in 2008, but in 2009 that slowed down. Between 2010 until 2013 Peru enjoyed very healthy GDP growth rate. In 2014, the GDP growth rate was a modest 2.38%, the following year it went up slightly to 3.35%, the trajectory continued in 2016 and Peru had a growth rate of 3.95%, but in 2017 it slowed down again with a growth rate of 2.53%.

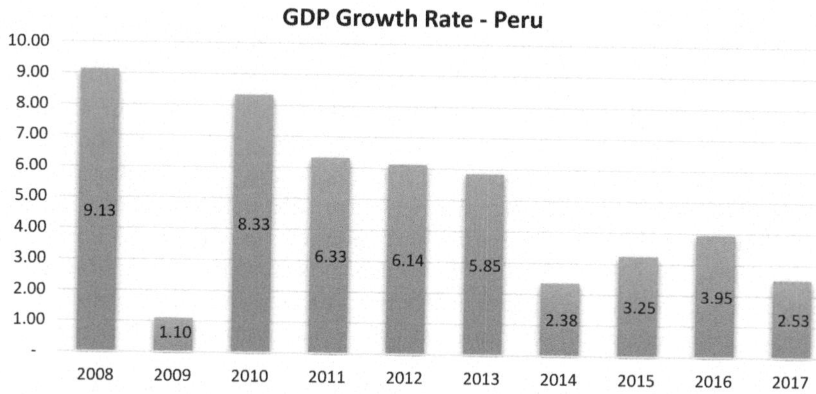

Fig. 6.4 The trend of Peru's GDP growth 2008–2017 (*Source* World Bank data 2019)

6.3 Monetary System—Inflation Targeting, Inflation, Financial Liberalization, and FDI Flow Patterns

6.3.1 Chile

A monetary system of country can be considered as the vehicle that transforms savings into investments (Amidu 2006). The Central Bank of Chile, an autonomous institution, takes charge of monetary and foreign exchange rate policies. The Central Bank of Chile is a major actor in this scenario and its tasks stabilize the inflation and maintain the normal flow of internal and external payments.

Until the early 1970s, Chile had a tightly regulated economy and financial system, with few links to international markets. The Pinochet regime opened financial markets broadly as part of radical monetarist economic experiment during its early years. In 1981, a sharp economic downturn and banking crisis pushed the government to close financial markets During the 1985–1990 period, as policymakers reopened markets but retained various capital controls to mitigate the dangers of short-term speculative capital movements, among them a ten-year minimum holding period for foreign investment (an exit barrier). The regulatory regime changed again after democratization in 1990, as policymakers eased controls on capital inflows and adopted an emphasis on restricting outflows.

The Central Bank of Chile switched to floating rate regime in 1999 abandoning its prolonged period of exchange rate band regime. The Central Bank of Chile took the decision to give more independence to monetary policy management and to cope with foreign shocks. The floating regime provided incentives to increase private sector international assets. It also expanded the exchange rate market and widened the use of risk coverage mechanisms. The Central Bank of Peru also took steps to develop domestic financial and foreign exchange markets that resulted in reducing the effect of banking concentration on monetary policy management as the exchange market widened.

Financial reform in Chile began in 1973. The reform included institutional, regulatory, and international aspects. By 1980, the process of liberalization was essentially completed. From 1981 onward, the changes were mostly responding to the growing imbalances.

The financial system was almost entirely under state control in late 1973. After a long period of mixed ownership, virtually all financial institutions had been nationalized during the period of 1970 through 1973. In 1974, Chile had 20 domestic nationalized commercial banks. In 1974, all but the Banco del Estado were sold to the private sector. In a year, the system became a predominantly private one, although the Banco del Estado has maintained a large and active presence. In 1974, the capital requirements for banks were increased to take account of past inflation. The maximum debt/capital ratio was maintained at 20, but noncompliance was penalized more strictly, at the rate of 2% daily on the excess debt.

Controls on interest rates were lifted in 1975. Pre-1975 the combination of interest rate ceilings and high inflation had consistently yielded negative real rates. This situation changed after liberalization. The idea was that positive real yields on domestic financial assets would reduce preferences for foreign or nonproductive assets. Indexed savings instruments and domestic dollar assets were aiding in this task. The attractiveness of domestic financial investments was also enhanced by changes in tax legislation. The tax legislation took account of inflation and ensured that thereafter only real interest earned counted as taxable income. Different kind of quantitative and selective controls on credit was also eliminated in 1975.

In 1976, the reserve requirement for banks was progressively reduced to 10% for sight deposits and 4% for time deposits, and interest payments on reserves were phased out. The objective was to reduce the cost to banks of holding required reserves. The required reserve could accumulate quite substantial under inflationary conditions. During the time the trend was to move toward multipurpose banking. In order to increase competition and lower costs, distinctions among commercial, investment, mortgage, and development activities were eliminated. Foreign banks were also allowed to open branches in Chile and to purchase Chilean banks. The result was rapid financial widening (Luders 1986).

The law that limited the maximum individual holdings of bank shares to 1.5% (for individuals) and to 3% (for firms and organizations) were abolished in 1978 because they had proved very difficult to enforce. In 1980, the treatment of bank borrowers was made more uniform, with regard to their credit limits in relation to bank capital and reserves. Previously, the legislation favored corporations over other organizations and individuals. The new regulation set a uniform limit at 5% for unsecured credits and at 25% for secured credits. These limits were halved in the case of borrowers linked to the bank.

In 1980, to facilitate underwriting operations, the limit on bank investment in a given enterprise's shares was increased from 10 to 20% of the bank's paid capital and reserves, but the limit of 10% of the firm's capital was maintained.

Limits on bank borrowing abroad were modified several times, and finally abolished in 1980.

These changes gave more freedom to the financial markets and placed more emphasis on rules than on the authorities' discretion in supervising the system.

Banks were allowed to borrow abroad in dollars but not to assume the exchange risk. The principal of the counterpart domestic loans had to be indexed to the exchange rate. There were also some limits on banks' foreign indebtedness as a percentage of capital and reserves.

The purpose of such restrictions was to ensure some control over domestic monetary policy. It was feared that, given very high domestic interest rates, total liberalization would induce huge and destabilizing capital inflows. Despite the restrictions on capital inflows, the inflows proved massive, as seen from Fig. 6.5 shows in part the policy of preannouncing the exchange rate until mid-1979, which made investing in Chile very appealing. Particularly massive inflows of capital occurred after the change in the exchange rate regime to fixed rates. The monetization of the ensuing reserve buildup was blamed for the slow progress in reducing inflation (Harberger 1985; Corbo and Sánchez 1985).

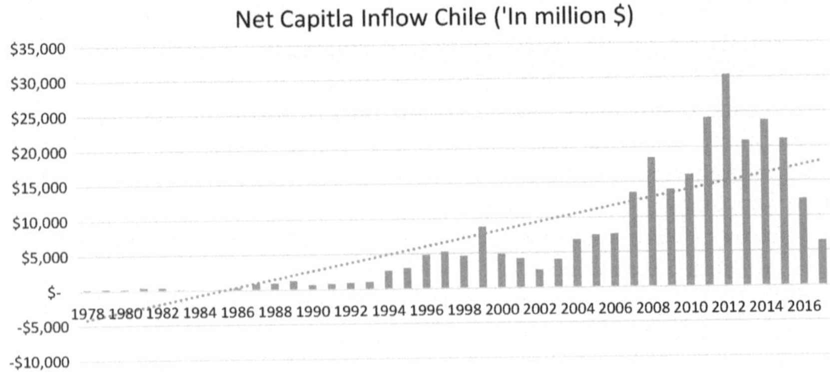

Fig. 6.5 The inflation rate of Chile 1981–2017 (*Source* World Bank data 2019)

In contrast to the situation in Brazil, Mexico, and other Latin American countries, the bulk of the borrowing in Chile was done by the private sector. 73.2% of net foreign debt had been incurred by the private sector. Financial institutions accounted for the lion's share of private external borrowing (72.9% of total inflows, private and public, in 1981).

Sweeping and thoroughgoing trade liberalization also was carried out by Chile. Quantitative controls were abolished and tariffs swiftly rationalized and lowered; by June 1979 a uniform tariff of 10% was in place. Both ex post and ex ante it has been argued that this sequence maximized the chances for adequate macroeconomic control (McKinnon 1982; Edwards 1984) has gone as far as to say that "Chile is to be treated as a norm or standard of reference" in this regard. But experts disagree on whether the speed and magnitude of the liberalization process were adequate.

Inflation rate for Chile has always been under control. Figure 6.6 shows that in 1985 inflation reached its peak at 30% mark. Since 1998 Chile is maintaining less than 5% inflation rate having very close to 0% inflation in 2009. In 2017 Chile had an impressive rate of 2.18% inflation rate.

Interest rate in Chile has been stable recently. Figure 6.7 shows that average discount rate has been 4.4%, recent money market rate is below 3%. Lending rate was on the higher spectrum in 2008 and 2012, but recently lending rate has been lower than 5%.

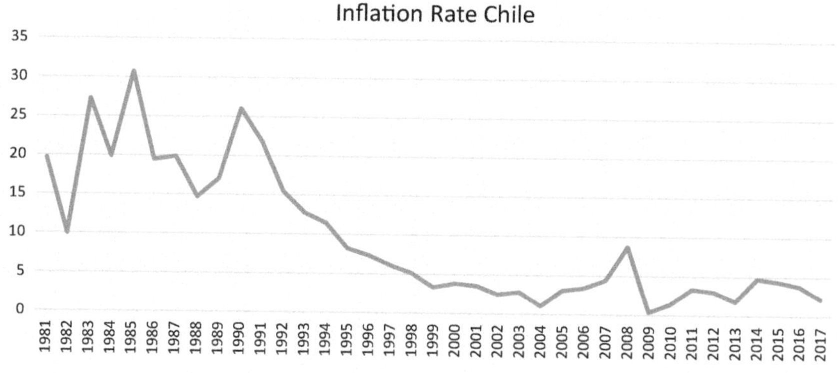

Fig. 6.6 The interest rate of Chile 2006–2018 (*Source* IMF data 2019)

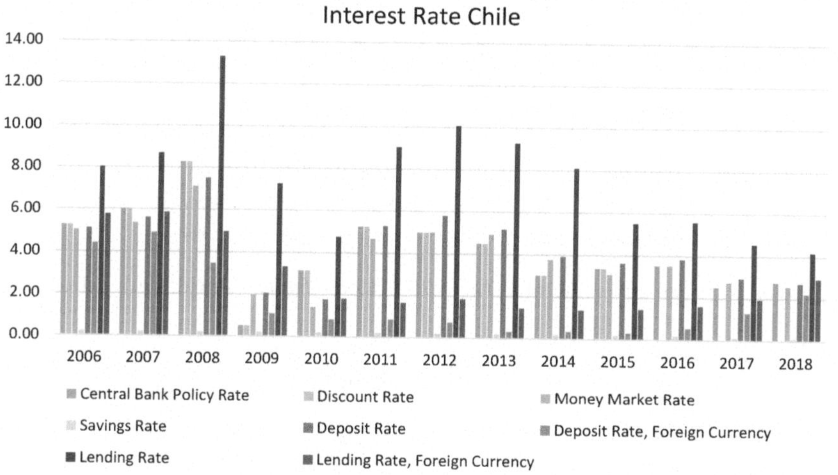

Fig. 6.7 Net capital inflow of Chile (*Source* International Monetary Fund data 2019)

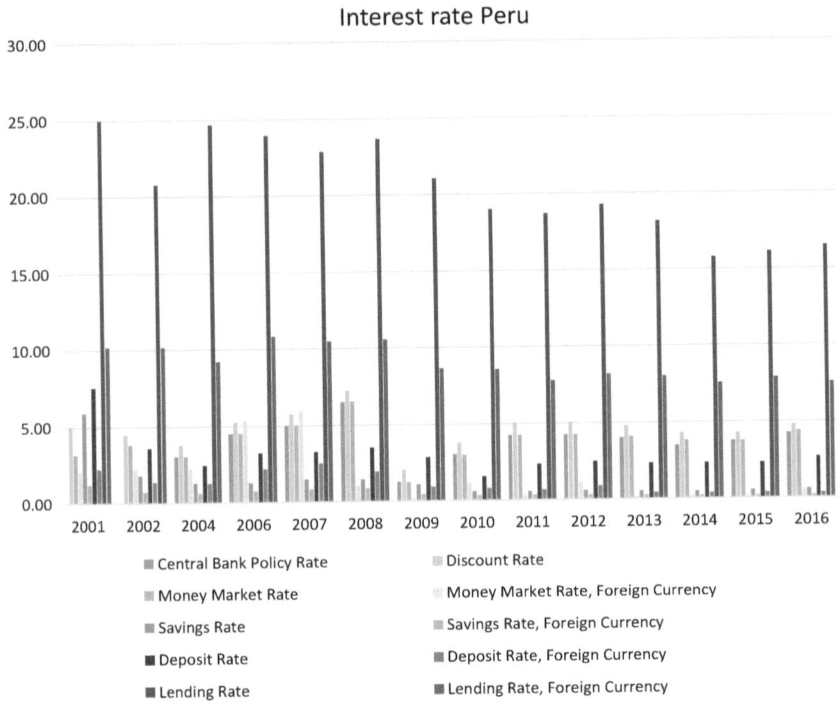

Fig. 6.8 The inflation rate of Peru's 1981–1995 (*Source* World Bank data 2019)

6.3.2 *Peru*

Central Bank of Peru (BCRP) is the center of monetary policy in Peru. The Central Bank, in May 2019, decided to keep the policy interest rate unchanged at an eight-year low of 2.75%. The main objective behind the monetary policy is to match market expectations. It last cut the policy interest rate in March 2019, by .25% that ended an easing cycle. Figure 6.8 shows the historic low policy rate for Peru was in 2009 at 1.25%.

Figure 6.9 shows Peru's battle with inflation in the 80s. In 1983 Peru had 111% inflation, in 1984 Peru had 110%, and the inflation rate climbed up in 1985 to an alarming 163%. In the following 2 years, the inflation rate remained below 100% but in 1988 saw the beginning of hyperinflation that forever put Peru on the history book. In 1988 Peru had 667% annual

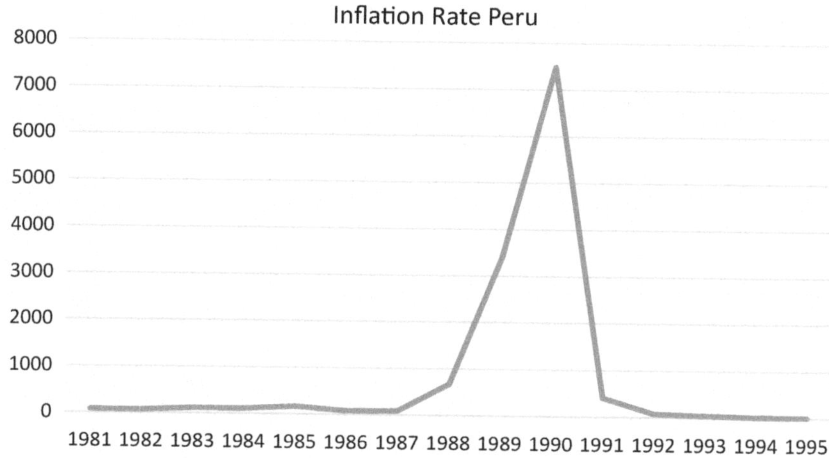

Fig. 6.9 The inflation rate of Peru's 1995–2017 (*Source* World Bank data 2019)

inflation, the following year in 1989 the hyperinflation rate reached 3398% annually and in 1990 the hyperinflation rate reached its peak 7481% annually. At some point during that time for 13 days, the daily rate of inflation was 5%. In 1991, the inflation rate was 409%, but the next year the rate dropped to 73%. Figure 6.10 shows that since 1995 inflation rate in Peru started to slow down from 11%. Since 1999 the inflation rate in Peru stayed below 3% rate annually.

The Central Bank of Peru is likely to maintain the current expansionary stance until both inflation and inflation expectations converge to the mid-point of the target range and economic growth approaches its potential.

The General attitude of Peruvian monetary policy includes liquidity and credit growth rates compatible with a consistent macroeconomic scenario and with the inflation objective set. In formulating the monetary policy, the Central Bank of Peru takes into account aggregate supply and demand trends. On the supply side, feasible growth rates by sector are factored in, identifying possible constraints or bottlenecks. On the demand side, consumption and investment growth in the public and private sectors are considered. The aim of monetary policy is to gradually achieve low international levels of inflation (once a single-digit level has been reached, the

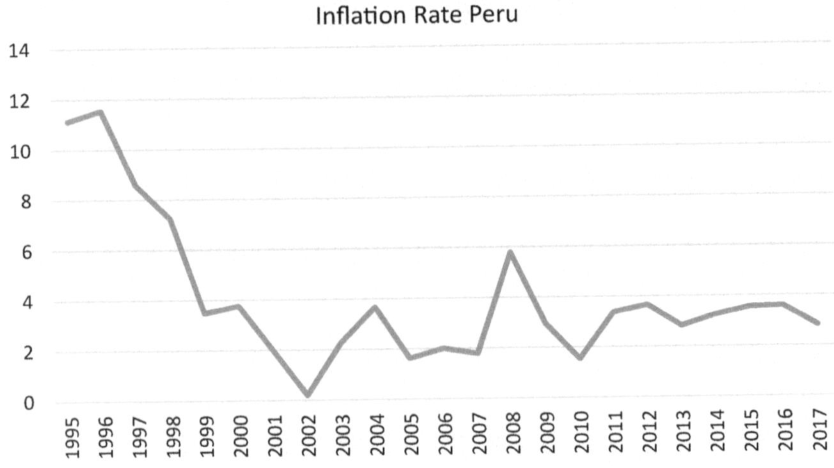

Fig. 6.10 The interest rate of Peru 2001–2016 (*Source* IMF data 2019)

speed of disinflation should be lower because of higher output costs) (De la Rocha 1998).

The Central Bank of Peru sets intermediate targets for base money growth consistent with its annual inflation targets. Base money targets are based on money demand forecasts. However, these targets are not made public, as changes in money demand might lead to their revision. Such changes could arise as a result of financial innovation or improvements in the payments system.

Targets for monetary aggregates are revised during the year if new information on a set of selected indicators suggests that money demand differs from the original forecast. According to De la Rocha (1998), the Central Bank of Peru examines the monetary stance by reference to the following indicators:

- the interbank interest rates
- the exchange rates
- projected inflation
- the fiscal stance
- aggregate demand
- credit to the private sector.

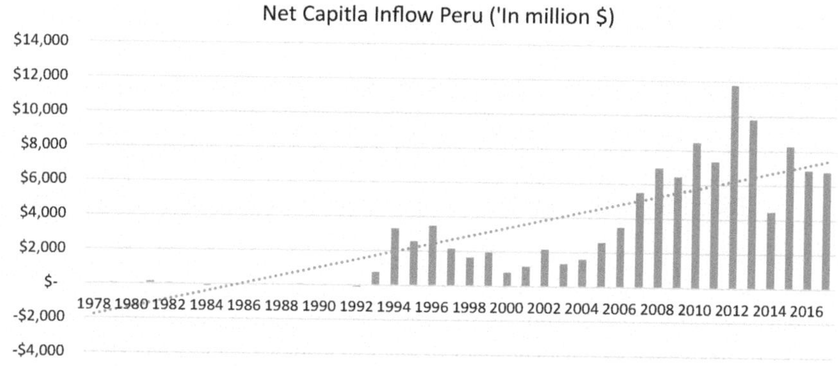

Fig. 6.11 Net capital inflow of Peru (*Source* International Monetary Fund Data 2019)

Large capital inflows constitute a challenge for monetary policy. Figure 6.11 shows Peru had increasing Capital inflows. They create pressure for an appreciation of the exchange rate and facilitate rapid credit expansion as external financing is readily available to domestic banks. Although over 70% of the inflows into Peru are long-term, the remaining 30% or so could be considered temporary. The potential volatility of these capital flows poses risk to macroeconomic stability and the health of the financial system. The Central Bank of Peru has chosen an active approach to dealing with them. To reduce the impact that capital flows have on the exchange rate and on aggregate demand, the Central Bank of Peru maintains the 45% marginal reserve requirement on foreign currency deposits. This also acts as a buffer stock against potential outflows and encourages holdings of domestic currency. Furthermore, the Bank sterilizes its net purchases of dollars in order to keep base money growth under control. Sterilization is carried out through sales of central bank CDs or through public sector deposits at the central bank.

Since the inflation was stabilized and economy was seeing rapid growth the need for further monetary easing was not a priority of the Central Bank of Peru. The economy did exceptionally well in 2018. However, growth likely also remains below potential, thus not exerting strong upward pressure on prices.

6.4 The Economic System: Typology of Economic Systems in the Region, Development of Nations, Demographic Trends, Evolving Comparative Advantage, Economic Transitions and Change—Informal Economy, Losses in Human Capital, Labor Market Protections, and Rigidities

Latin American economies have enjoyed a decent economic growth in the past decade. Compared to the developed region. But they are lagging behind in growth of other developing countries. The growth in Latin American counties is facing threat from various factors including decline in fertility rates, an end of commodity book and the risk of increased protectionism. That is why the economic objective of Latin American countries need to forge a broad agenda that removes obstacles to competitiveness, promotes the adoption of digital and automation technologies, addresses labor market pressures, and raises investment in long-term drivers of productivity.

6.4.1 Chile

After the trade liberalization of the 1970s, Chile experienced a substantial increase in productivity. In the 1987–1991 period, Chile's productivity increased much more than that of any other country in Latin America. Chile's national accounts have been impressive for quite some time. During 1970s, the share of GDP generated by agriculture, livestock, and forestry had been in the neighborhood of 7%. In the next 30 years, this contribution has increased just a fraction of a percentage. For the vast majority of countries, as income and output expand and national economies become more developed, this sector generates a smaller share of GDP. In the case of Chile, the absence of this phenomenon is present. Elimination of discrimination against export agriculture that had characterized the Chilean economy during the decades of import substitution industrialization. As a result, the level of productivity of the agricultural sector had increased significantly by the early 1990s. This might be the reason why Chile did not see much decline in the share of GDP generated by agriculture, livestock, and forestry.

Manufacturing sector represents approximately 21% of GDP for Chile. This was significantly lower than this sector's share of total output in early 70s, when it was almost 25%. This reduction in participation can be attributed to structural reforms in 80s that eliminated the protection walls that had artificially encouraged Chile's industrial sector during the 1960s.

The share of mining in GDP remained roughly constant over the period. However, the composition of mining production changed a lot. Copper in particular saw a drop in the importance. The share of services increased from the neighborhood of 26 to 29% in the past 30 years. Significant increase took place in financial sector.

6.4.2 *Income Distribution*

Based on OECD income inequality data, Income distribution of Chile is consistent with the income distribution of rest of Latin America that has traditionally one the most unequal income distributions in the world. During the years of military rule, income inequality increased significantly in Chile. In 1985 about 25% of households lived in extreme poverty, and that 45% of households lived below the poverty line. During the 1990–1993 period, the incidence of poverty declined substantially. In late 1993, the Ministry of Planning and Cooperation estimated that between 1990 and 1993 more than 1.3 million people moved out of poverty. This was the result of the rapid rate of growth experienced by the economy; and the implementation of social programs aimed at the poorest groups in society. The social programs were designed to deliver directly to the poor, avoid leakages to middle- and upper-income groups. These programs have been largely successful. The basic housing program was reformed in the early 1980s, more than 50% of the subsidies reached the poorest three deciles of the population. In 1969, before the system was reformed, only 20% of subsidies were received by the poorest 30% of the population. Chile made significant stride in reducing income gap.

6.4.3 *Trade Policy*

Between 1950 and 1970, Chile went through three attempts at trade liberalization without ever reaching full liberalization. All three attempts quickly ended in frustration and in a reversion to exchange controls, the use of multiple exchange rates, and massive quantitative restrictions. All collapsed, at least in part because of a highly overvalued real exchange rate. In 1974, Chile adopted singly an open trade regime characterized by low uniform import tariffs, a lack of exchange or trade controls, and minimum restrictions on capital movements. Starting in 1979, Chile's trade policy became highly liberalized; subsequently, there were no quantitative restrictions, licenses, or prohibitions. A uniform import tax varying between 10 and 35% took effect, and, until 1980, Chile avoided real exchange rate overvaluation. By 1990 Chile was the only country, according to the World Bank, whose index of liberalization reached the maximum possible level of 20, indicating an absence of external sector distortions.

In 1973 import tariffs averaged 105% and were highly dispersed, with some goods subject to nominal tariffs of more than 700% and others fully exempted from import duties. In addition to tariffs, a series of quantitative restrictions were applied, including outright import prohibitions and prior import deposits of up to 10,000%. These protective measures were complemented by a highly distorting multiple exchange rate system consisting of fifteen different nominal exchange rates. By August 1975, all quantitative restrictions had been eliminated, and the average tariff had been reduced to 44%. This process of tariff reductions continued until June 1979, when all tariffs but one (that on automobiles) were set at 10%. The authorities adopted a fixed exchange rate policy that resulted in a critical overvaluation of the Chilean peso. This was a huge loss in international competitiveness of Chile and cause a deep crisis in 1982. In 1984–1985 this situation was reversed, and a policy of a depreciated and highly competitive real exchange rate was implemented. Low tariffs and a competitive real exchange rate had a significant impact on Chile's economic structure. Productivity in tradable sectors grew substantially, and exports became highly diversified. Chile had also diversified its export markets, with the result that no individual market bought more than 20% of the country's total exports. By the early 1990s, exports had become the engine of growth, and the Chilean trade reform was winning praise from multinational institutions and observers of different ideological persuasions. Largely thanks to the boom in exports between 1986 and 1991, particularly, based on World Bank data, the increasing growth in exports of fresh fruits and manufactured products, Chile experienced the highest rate of GDP growth in Latin America, with an annual increase of 4.2%. The successive administrations decided to continue the opening process and reduced import tariffs to a uniform 11% (USTR.gov).

6.4.4 Unions and Labors

Chile reluctantly accepted the Labor Plan in 1979 but unions did not become active until the early 1980s. The union was able to push for wage concessions during the economic boom of that period. A minority maintained a tough stance in opposition to the new system, but they lacked significant influence, so opposition eventually disappeared. The reforms of 1990–1991 represented a moderate increase in workers' bargaining power in each of the three central areas of the labor law: dismissals; the right to collective bargaining; and the right of employers to hire temporary replacements or to impose lockouts during strikes. The Labor Plan had introduced the practice of dismissals without cause and established a severance pay equal to one month's salary per year of service up to a maximum of five months' worth, this reform reinstated the principle of dismissal only with cause, and it increased the severance pay ceiling to eleven months. The law gave the employer the right to limit to thirty-five days the period of bargaining with all unions representing the enterprises' workers. Collective agreements can establish pay scales, indexation formulas, fringe benefits, and the like, but they cannot limit the sovereignty of the employer over the organization and administration of the enterprise according to those laws.

According to the law, a strike would suspend the individual contract, give employers a conditional right to temporary replacement, and give employees a conditional right to renounce union membership and return to work. Employers can use temporary replacements from the first day of the strike if their last offer, before the strike was declared, was equivalent to the previous contract adjusted by the consumer price index.

Workers have almost doubled their participation in labor unions since 1983, and by 1990 about 13% of those employed were affiliated with unions. During 1990, 25,000 workers, out of 184,000 who participated in collective contracts, used strikes as a means of pressing their demands. Most strikes during 1990 and 1991 were of short duration (Scully 1992).

6.4.5 Peru

Historically, the great majority of the Peruvian population depended on agriculture and lived in the countryside. In 1876, Lima was the only Peruvian city with over 100,000 people accounting for only 4% of the population. Peru maintained an open economic system with little government intervention and few restrictions on either imports or foreign investment.

This investment became instrumental in the twentieth century in the extraction of raw materials for export (Scully 1992).

For many Latin American countries, the impact of falling export prices and curtailed external credit in the Great Depression of the 1930s led to fundamental changes in economic policies. Many governments began to raise protection against imports in order to stimulate domestic industry and to take more active roles in shaping economic change. But Peru held back from this common move and kept on with a relatively open economy. That put it behind many other countries in post-World War II industrialization and led to increasing pressures for change. Significant protection started in the 1960s, accompanied by both new restrictions on foreign investment and a more active role of government in the economy.

Peru's most famous exports have been gold, silver, and guano. Its gold was taken out on a large scale by the Spanish for many years following the conquest and is of little significance now, but silver remains an important export. Guano served as Europe's most important fertilizer in the mid-nineteenth century and made Peru for a time the largest Latin American exporter to Europe. The guano boom ran out about 1870, after generating a long period of exceptional economic growth. When the guano boom ended, the economy retreated temporarily but then recovered with two new directions for expansion. One was a new set of primary product exports and the other a turn toward more industrial production for the domestic market.

The alternative primary exports that initially replaced guano included silver, cotton, rubber, sugar, and lead. Industrial products remained notably absent from Peru's list of exports until the 1970s. Manufactured goods were only 1% of total exports during that time. Peru began a process of import substitution industrialization combined with stronger incentives for exports. Domestic entrepreneurs responded successfully, and the economy began to show promising signs of more diversified and autonomous growth.

Peru made an early recovery of some of its main exports in the 1930s, and then by development of new primary exports in the early post-World War II period, Peru became the most successful economy in Latin America up to the mid-1960s. But increasing pressure on the land from a rapidly growing population, accompanied by rising costs and limited supplies of some of the country's natural resources, began to intensify demands for change. Peru welcomed foreign investment and, in some periods, adopted tax laws specifically designed to encourage it.

The deterioration of the economy led some companies to withdraw and held foreign investment down to very low levels through the 1980s (Alvarado et al. 2017). The redirection of economic strategy under the Fujimori government in 1990–1991 included a return to welcoming conditions for foreign investment, providing a much more favorable legal context, and disavowing completely the control-oriented policies of the governments of Velasco and García. Several foreign oil companies responded immediately, although the disorganized state of the economy and the context of political violence discouraged any general inflow of new foreign investment. Much of the impetus for economic growth came from primary exports.

6.4.6 Income Distribution

The distribution of income in Peru has been unequal for some time. The degree of inequality apparently decreased between 1970 and 1985. The dominant causes of inequality before World War II were a very high concentration of ownership of land and access to capital and to education. The sociopolitical structure that condemned the indigenous rural population to bare sustenance with little chance of mobility also contributed to income inequality. Since the 1960s, access to education gradually has spread to rural areas, and increased migration to the cities opened up new opportunities for people previously blocked in poverty-stricken rural occupations. The Agrarian Reform Law of 1969 wiped out large private land holdings and led in the 1980s to a vastly less unequal distribution of individual ownership. The rise of production and export of coca played a role in raising rural incomes in the 1980s. The proportion of the rural population below the poverty line fell from 68% in 1970 to 64% by 1986. The proportion of urban families was rising from 28 to 45% at the same time. The positive change for rural families was small, and the negative change for urban families was large, but because urban poverty was initially less the degree of inequality between the rural and urban sectors decreased (Mayer 2009).

During the period of exceptional economic growth from 1961 to 1972, the incomes of the poorest 60% of Peruvian families increased at a rate of 2.3% a year. As growth weakened from the mid 1970s, both average real wages and minimum real wages began a prolonged decline, and total wages fell relative to incomes of property owners. But earnings of the lowest income groups in agriculture went up, slightly reducing the percentage of rural families falling below the poverty line. A World Bank study concludes that these changes reduced the degree of inequality between 1972 and

1985. Based on OECD income inequality data the share of the poorest 60% increase from 18 to 27% of total income.

An alternative measure of inequality, the Gini index, shows a similar improvement. The higher the coefficient, the higher the degree of inequality. Based on World Bank data, in the early 1960s and again in the early 1970s, Peru had either the highest or the second highest Gini coefficient for all the Latin American countries measured, at 0.61 for 1961 and 0.59 for 1972. By 1985 it had come down to 0.47, far below Brazil and only slightly higher than Colombia. These countries all have high inequality by world standards, but by 1985 Peru no longer stood out as the worst.

Based on the latest estimate available inequality in distribution for Peru had increased slightly compared with 1980s, with the Gini coefficient stands at 43 (world Bank Estimate 2018). It would not mean much to reduce inequality if that just meant more equal sharing of greater poverty. The one clearly positive combination of indicators is that the incidence of poverty fell, if only slightly, for the rural households who have always constituted the majority of Peru's poor.

6.4.7 *Unions and Labors*

Organized labor normally did not have much bargaining power in Peru. Peruvian labor has never been more than moderately organized. Unionization did not take off significantly until the political climate changed with the reformist military government of 1968. Labor has played a more active political role than being able to prevent deterioration of real wages.

Organized labor in Peru got off to a slow start in Peru compared with active unionism in Argentina, Chile, and Venezuela. Still, the textile workers, in the one sizeable industry of the time, managed to defy the government and win a famous strike in 1919. They gave the credit to a student activist who stepped into lead them and negotiated an impressive victory. After the military government took power in 1968, unionization spread rapidly. More new unions were given legal recognition from 1968 to 1978 than in all prior Peruvian history. There were 2152 recognized unions in 1968 and 4500 by 1978. The new unions began to strike out more on their own to undertake joint negotiations and demonstrations with community groups of all kinds.

In the economic contraction following 1975, labor played a more active role in social protest than ever before. The first general strike in the country's history, in July 1977, seemed to herald a new era in labor relations in Peru. Organized labor certainly did not stop the devastating fall of real wages in the 1980s. Still, average wages for workers under collective bargaining contracts have been much higher than those for workers without them. Looking into the market today, the average wage for those with contracts is 2.2 times that of workers without them (Posner 2008).

6.5 Commercial System—Free Trade Blocs, Bilateral Investment Treaties, Investor-State Dispute Settlements, and Investment Incentives

6.5.1 Chile

Chile is an attractive destination for investors who are looking for an open market, strong institutions and rule of law. Chile has a legal framework to attract and protect foreign Direct Investment. Chile created Foreign Direct Investment Protection Agency (APIE) in 2015. APIE provides service to FDI in four categories: attraction, pre-investment, landing, and aftercare. Chile has very few restrictions on FDI. Regulatory system in Chile is very transparent. The transfer policies of Chile are very developed. Chile has many bilateral investment agreements and free trade agreements with United States and Europe. Private Property rights and Foreign ownership and investment are respected in Chile except mineral and fossil fuel. Intellectual Property rights are generally respected. Compare to other Latin American countries corruption is minimal in Chile. Transparency Internal ranked Chile 24 out of 176 countries in 2016. World Bank ranked Chile 59 out of 190 in World Bank's "Ease of doing business" ranking in 2016.

6.5.2 Free Trade Block

Chile has 2 free trade zones: one is in the northern port city of Iquique (Tarapaca Region) and the other is in the far south port city of Punta Arenas (Magallanes Region). Traders and producers in these zones are exempt from corporate income tax, value added tax, and customs duties. Only exception is mining, fishing, and financial services. Foreign-owned firms have similar investment opportunities in these zones as firms from Chile.

6.5.3 *Bilateral Investment Treaties*

Chile signed 55 Bilateral Investment Treaties with Argentina, Australia, Austria, Belgium and Luxembourg, Bolivia, Finland, France, Germany, Greece, Guatemala, Honduras, Iceland, Italy, Malaysia, Nicaragua, Norway, Panama, Paraguay, Peru, Philippines, Poland, Portugal, Romania, South Korea, Spain, Sweden, Switzerland, Ukraine, the United Kingdom, Uruguay, and Venezuela. Chile has free trade agreement with United States.

6.5.4 *Investor-State Dispute Settlement*

Chile became a member of International Center for Settlement of Investment Disputes (ICSID) in 1991. In 1997 Chile signed the convention on the Recognition and Enforcement of Foreign Arbitral Awards (New York Convention) in 1958. Chile is also party to Pan-American Convention on Private International Law, Inter-American Convention on International Commercial Arbitration, Washington on the Settlement of Investment Disputes between states and National of other states.

Over the past ten years, there was only one investment dispute brought by a foreign investor that resulted in foreign arbitral awards. There is no history of extrajudicial action against foreign investors. Overall there is no reasonable fear exist in terms of investing in Chile.

6.5.5 *Investment Incentives*

There are many incentives to different geographical zones to the information technology sector. These benefits include cofinancing of feasibility studies, incentives for the purchase of land, hiring local labor, facilitation, project financing, etc.

Chile has incentive programs to promote investment and employment in remote region as well as other areas that suffer from poverty. These incentives include tax holiday and subsidies. These incentives are open to foreign firms.

Chile started "Start-UP Chile" program in 2011 that gives $40,000 USD grant to selected entrepreneurs and Chilean work visa to develop a "Start-Up" business in Chile. As of today, 1309 startups were helped through this program (Forbes November 2019).

6.5.6 *Peru*

Peru was one of the fastest growing Latin American economies between 2004 and 2013. Peru maintained almost 6% growth rate per year during that period. Since 2014 the growth rate slowed down. The driving force behind the growth is countercyclical stimulus spending, consumption, and private investment. In 2016, private investment value was 36 billion USD. Peru signed several free rade agreements recently to encourage integrations with global economy. In 2009, Peru signed Trade Promotion Agreement (PTPA) with United States.

Peru has few negative factors that impact its investment. Corruption is a sticking thorn for Peru. In 2016 Transparency International ranked Peru 101 out of 176 countries in its corruption perception Index. Brazilian company Odebrecht confessed to having paid US$29 million in bribes in Peru in 2016. That lead to investigations involving high-level officials of the last three Peruvian administration and a shutdown of major infrastructure projects. Civil unrest is another actor that negatively affects Peru's investment environment. There have been at least 155 active social conflicts in Peru as of 2017 as reported by Ombudsman (Haslam and Tanimoune 2016).

Mining industries are the key to foreign investment in Peru. In 2016, 23% of the Foreign Direct Investment went to mining sector according to Private Investment Promotion Agency (Pro-Inversion). 20% of the Foreign Direct Investment went to communication section, 17% went to financial sector, 14% went to Energy and 13% went to industry (Alvarado et al. 2017).

6.5.7 *Free Trade Block*

According to Export.gov Peru has two types of trade zones. The first one is export, transformation, industry, trade and services zones (CETICOS) and the second one is free trade zone (ZOFRATACNA) in Tacna. The rules and tax benefits to the zones are exactly same for foreign and national investors. These zones couldn't attract enough foreign investment.

6.5.8 *Bilateral Investment Treaties*

According to Export.gov Peru has 30 bilateral investment agreement's Peru has free trade agreements with Canada, Chile, China, Colombia,

Costa Rica, The European Free Trade Association, Honduras, Japan, Mexico, Panama, Singapore, South Korea, and Thailand. The United States and Peru have Promotion Agreement (PTPA) that includes investment provision between United States and Peru. Peru has Framework Agreement with MERCOSUR countries (Argentina, Brazil, Paraguay, Uruguay, and Venezuela), as well as, a partial preferential agreement with Cuba.

Peru has bilateral Investment agreements with Argentina, Australia, Belgium-Luxembourg, Bolivia, Canada, Chile, China, Colombia, Cuba, Czech Republic, Denmark, Paraguay, Portugal, Romania, Spain, Sweden, Switzerland, Thailand, the United Kingdom, and Venezuela.

6.5.9 *Investor-State Dispute Settlement*

Peru signed 1958 Convention on Recognition and Enforcement of Foreign Arbitral Awards (New York Convention). Peru also is a party to the International Center for Settlement of Investment Disputes (ICSID convention). However, dispute between foreign investors and Government of Peru regarding preexisting contracts needs to enter national courts, unless otherwise permitted. There are some private organizations such as American Chamber of Commerce, the Lima Chamber of Commerce, and Universidad Catholica, which operate as private arbitration center.

Trade Promotion Agreement (PTPA) provides investor-state claim mechanisms. It does not require investor to go through all the local judicial remedies or administrative process before filing a claim. The investor can choose to file a claim under different arbitral mechanisms including ICSID convention and international trade Law Arbitration rules. There have been few claims that were filled recently. There is no recent history of extrajudicial action against foreign investors.

6.5.10 *Investment Incentives*

Peru offers foreign investors legal and tax stability agreements to stimulate private investment. The benefit of this agreement is that it guarantees that the statutes on income taxes, remittances, export promotion regimes, administrative procedures, and labor hiring regimes in effect at the time of investment contact will remain unchanged for that investment for 10 years. In order to qualify, investment need to exceed US$10 million in the mining and hydrocarbons sector of US$5 million within 2 years in another sector. An agreement to acquire more that 50% of a company's share in the privatization process will also qualify an investor for a legal or tax stability agreement as long as the company agrees to expand the installed capacity of the company or enhance its technological development (Alvarado et al. 2017).

6.6 Capital Market—Stock Market Structure, IPOs, Institutional Investors, Monetary Stimulus

6.6.1 Chile

The stock market has shown progress in Chile over the past 20 years. The recession of 1982 instigated reforms that led to a robust system and reduced risk. In order to increase the protection of minority shareholders, the OPAS law was enacted in 2001. OPAS law is the key to the transparency of the capital market. Subsequently, further reforms to encourage savings and attract foreign investors led to a vigorous development of mutual funds and the Pension Fund Administrators (AFP) in Chile.

The main trading center of Chile is the Santiago Stock Exchange. In 2008, 86.6% of the local market was centralized and the amount of securities transactions reached US$31,790 million.

More than 150 companies regularly list their shares on the Santiago Stock Market. The index of most traded shares is the IPSA (Selective Price Index Shares), which considers the 40 actions with the most movement. Despite the complex global economic situation between January and February of 2009, the Santiago Stock Exchange showed a rise of 3.9% and is ranked among the most profitable in the world, only surpassed in Latin America by Caracas Stock Exchange. Figure 6.12 shows that in 2010 Chile saw the highest stock market trading volume amounting US$57 billion. The number dropped since then. In 2018, the trading volume is standing at US$48 billion. Figure 6.12 shows that since 2010 trading volume as a percentage of GDP has sharply declined in Chile.

Turnover ratio is the value of domestic shares traded divided by their market capitalization. The value is annualized by multiplying the monthly average by 12. Figure 6.13 shows that turnover ratio climbed up since 2001 but decline since 2010 and then climbed back up since 2015.

The privatization of the pension system, with the subsequent creation of the AFP, is one of the most innovative reforms in the economic history of Chile and the world. People can choose between five administrators to manage their savings. By law, AFP collects 10% of gross wages paid, money

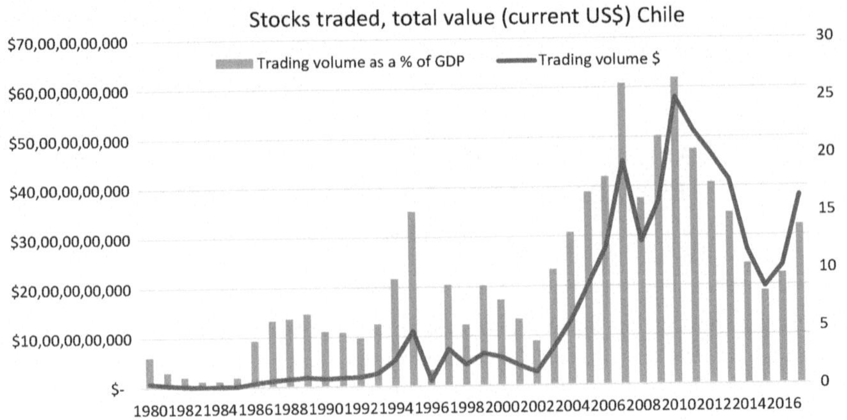

Fig. 6.12 Stock trading in Chile (*Source* International Monetary Fund data 2019)

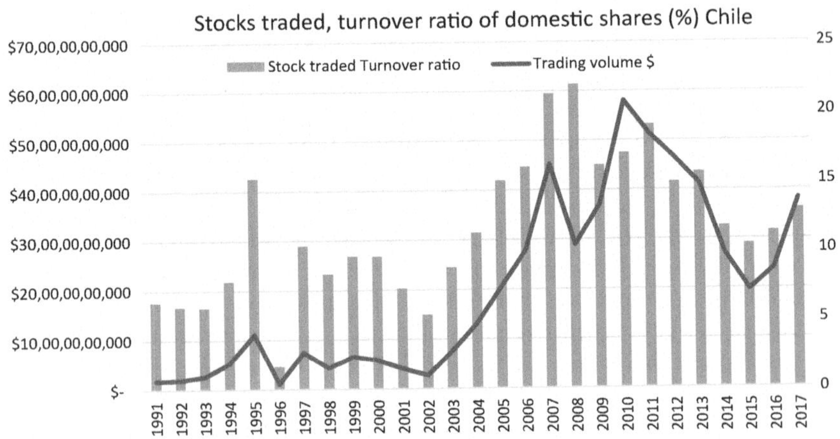

Fig. 6.13 Stock traded turnover ratio in Chile (*Source* International Monetary Fund data 2019)

that goes to individual investment accounts and are divided between fixed and variable income funds. The money is invested in various economic sectors, including infrastructure and telecommunications.

6.6.2 *Initial Public Offering (IPO)*

Chilean underwriters have adopted international standards for conducting IPOs only recently. The first underwriting process with a formal Information Memorandum and organized sale efforts appeared only in October of 1991. Since then and until May 1997, 43 private companies went public using underwriting services from investment bankers, stock houses or commercial banks. Our paper documents the Chilean IPO market development during these six years and how it is related to structural changes in the Chilean capital market. It may be useful for academics, practitioners, and regulators of other countries to examine this evolution (Celis and Maturana 1998).

The way of going public in Chile determines that IPO shares are not always sold in just one day. In some cases, placement takes even several weeks. This makes it difficult to obtain a single issuing price and to determine the proceeds collected. In the case of slow placements (several weeks) indicate that part of the shares may have been placed at prices higher than the first trading day's average price. The "money on the table" left by the issuer could exist.

The Best Efforts system used in Chile and the tax advantages of new stock issues could be the reason for the lower level of underpricing. The "Winner's Curse" hypothesis and the legal liability argument seem to have little applicability in the Chilean IPO issuance case—reinforcing the lower underpricing. Underwriter reputation plays a key role in determining short-run underpricing. Underwriters that finally dominate the market are the long-term players

6.6.3 *Institutional Investors*

The Chilean institutional investors developed as part of a series of macroeconomic and financial sector reforms that targeted both the demand and supply side of capital. On the demand side, Chile has introduced reforms to foster capital market development. Corporations and the government have then issued a wide range of securities, including long-term local currency bonds. Moreover, Chile's stable macroeconomic performance since

Table 6.7 Institutional investors in Chile

Institutional investor	*Sample period*	*Frequency*	*No. of OBS*	*No. of funds/companies*
Chilean domestic mutual funds	January 2002–December 2009	Monthly	965,209	86
Chilean insurance companies	January 2002–December 2008	Monthly	4,061,927	36
Chilean PFAs	January 2002–June 2008	Monthly	6,659,681	45
Chilean PFAs	July 1996–July 2008	Daily	201,288,833	62
US mutual funds	2003–2005	Annually	3816	167

Source Superintendence of Securities and Insurance in Chile

the early 1990s and its long history of issuing inflation-linked instruments have also reduced the risk and the cost of long-term assets (Table 6.7).

Mutual funds, pension funds, and insurance companies collectively had assets under management equivalent to 84% of GDP. They have played an important role in financial markets, investing in different types of asset classes, such as bonds, deposits, equities, mortgages, and money market instrument, issued by both the private and the public sectors, domestically and abroad. Given their size and importance as conduits of savings, these institutional investors have offered different products and have been subject to different regulations.

Pension funds are the most important institutional investor in Chile, with assets under management equivalent to 56% of GDP. Life insurance companies managed assets equivalent to 18% of GDP. These assets come mainly from funds accumulated by pensioners seeking an annuity income during their retirement period of around 20 years. Given the long-term nature of their liabilities, insurance companies have strong incentives to hedge their liabilities with long-maturity bonds to reduce their default risk and increase customers' demand. Mutual funds are the institutional investor less exposed to regulatory requirements to structure their portfolios. In general, regulation is flexible and is mainly focused on diversification and disclosure requirements (Opazo et al. 2014).

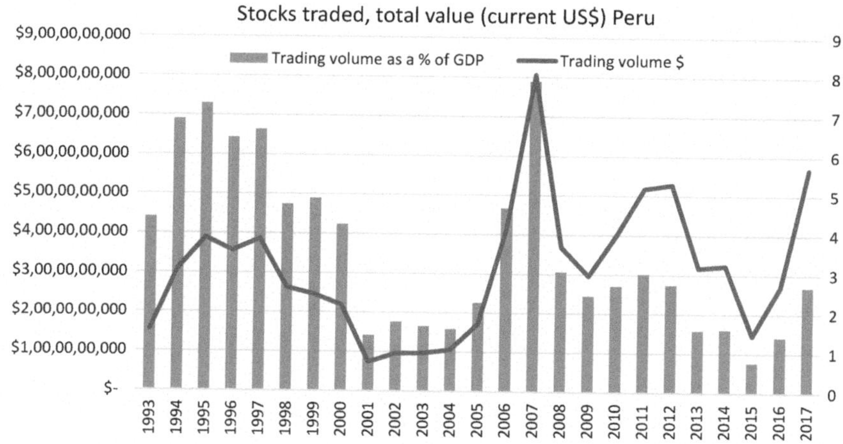

Fig. 6.14 Net stock trading in Peru (*Source* International Monetary Fund data 2019)

6.6.4 Peru

Based on IMF data Peruvian Stock Exchange is the 41st largest exchange out of the 110 stock exchanges in the world. The Bolsa de Valores de Lima's Market Capitalization is $100.42 Billion adjusted US Dollars as of March 2019. Although the primary currency used by the Bolsa de Valores de Lima is the Peru Sol.

Market Capitalization to GDP ratio, which when compared to the historic ratio is an indicator that a market is over or undervalued, is 47.75%. Figure 6.14 shows that Bolsa de Valores de Lima's Market trading volume reached US$8 billion mark in 2007, since then the trading volume dropped, but as a percentage of GDP the trading volume has been climbing upwards since 2015.

The Lima Stock Exchange (LSE), known locally by its Spanish acronym BVL, has recently begun diversifying beyond its century-plus history heavy on mining company listings in mineral- and metal-rich Peru. Following the introduction of electronic trading earlier this decade, the LSE's market capitalization expanded rapidly and trading volumes and value continue to grow impressively.

The LSE was first formed in 1860 and then reformed in 1898 as the Stock Exchange of Lima following a period of hyperinflation that knocked

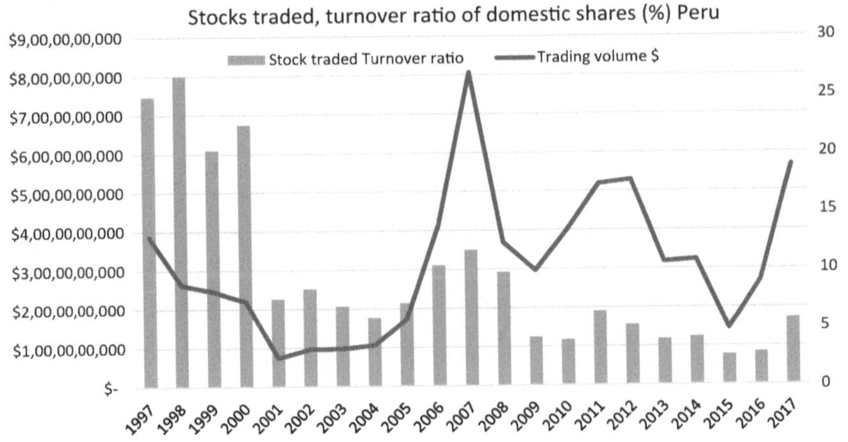

Fig. 6.15 Stock traded turnover ratio in Peru (*Source* International Monetary Fund data 2019)

out the previous exchange. Following the upheavals of previous decades, the renewed Bolsa de Comercio de Lima began trading in 1951, replaced in 1971 by the modern-day LSE. The LSE later adopted an electronic trading platform and in 2002 moved to transform the exchange into a corporation commencing 2003. Consequently, the Inter-American Development Bank reports that the total market capitalization of the LSE's listed companies grew six times in the six years to 2007, to almost US$108 billion.

Turnover ratio is the value of domestic shares traded divided by their market capitalization. The value is annualized by multiplying the monthly average by 12. Figure 6.15 shows that the turnover ratio started going up since 2003 reached its pick in 2007 and since then it was a seesaw. In 2017 the turnover ratio is over 5.

In September 2009 the LSE joined the Colombia Stock Exchange and the Santiago Stock Exchange in Chile in agreeing to integrate their stock market trading and memberships [3]. The LSE also recently announced a partnership with the Inter-American Development Bank's Multilateral Investment Fund (MIF) to encourage smaller Chilean companies, preferably one located in rural areas, to list on the LSE by offering assistance and support from the IPO process.

The LSE's benchmark stock index, the Lima General Index—ticker symbol IGBVL—was formed on December 31, 1981 with a base value of 100. The IGBVL is value-weighted, tracks the largest and most traded stocks on the LSE and was valued in mid-September 2009 at around 15,000 Peruvian nuevo sol (PEN) (Trading economics).

6.6.5 IPO

In Peru, public offering of securities offer is directed to the general public or to a determined segment of noninstitutional investors for the purchase, sale or placement of securities. In Peru, every offer is presumed public if it is addressed to more than one hundred (100) prospective investors. However, Peruvian legislation provides for certain safe harbors, and deems as private offers (i.e. not a public offering) those that are directed to institutional investors or those in which the lowest unitary value of the offered securities equals or exceeds a figure indexed to inflation (equivalent to approximately S/. 450,000 for 2012). Securities that are subject to this kind of offer shall be registered in the SMPR, for which, an Information Memorandum, financial statements from the latest two (2) fiscal years and certain other documents and information described in the applicable regulation shall be filed with the SMV. The Information Memorandum contains information such as the characteristics of the securities being offered, rights and obligations to be granted to investors, relevant risk factors, issuer's financial statements, information about the structuring entity and the placement agent, the placement procedure and other information considered material by the issuer and the structuring entity (Sustainable Stock exchange initiative) [http://www.sseinitiative.org].

6.6.6 Institutional Investor

In Peru, there are two pension systems. However, in both cases, the worker must be at least 65 years old in order to apply for retirement pension, and must have contributed for the minimum number of years. In special cases, both the retirement age and the longevity requirement may be reduced as a result of high-risk activities performed by workers, who may then receive their retirement pension at an earlier age. (1) National Pension System. The National Pension System is a system administered by the government through the Office of Pensions. All workers subject to labor regulations in the private sector must adhere to such system, unless they are affiliated with

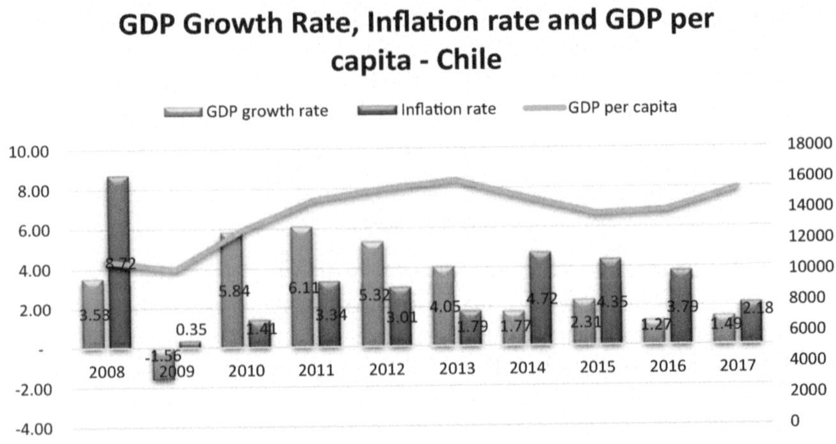

Fig. 6.16 Macroeconomic indicators of Chile (*Source* World Bank data 2019)

the private pension system. (2) Private Pension System. Workers subject to labor regulations in the private sector may choose to be affiliated with the private pension system administered by private pension fund managers.

6.7 Discussion

6.7.1 Chile

Chile has long been showcased as an economic darling. Following are the strength of Chili's Economy

- Macroeconomic stability, growth perspective, and low level of risk (Fig. 6.16).
- A top Latin American importer per capita enjoys excellent solvency.
- High purchasing power (for Latin America).
- Wealth of natural resources (copper, agriculture, fishery, and forestry resources).
- Internationalized Chilean companies.
- Labor laws that tend to be favorable toward business, mainly due to the flexibility of working hours and uncomplicated procedures for the dismissal of employees.

- Foreign companies can also benefit from privileged access to regional markets through different free trade agreements.
- Various free trade agreements.
- Flexible monetary, fiscal, and exchange rate policies.
- Favorable business climate, political, and institutional stability.
- Member of the OECD and the Pacific Alliance.

The road of Chile's economy has some speed bump. Careful and prudent manner of addressing them will ensure that economic success will continue. Here are some of the weakness of Chile's economy.

- Lack of innovation, very weak spending in research and development.
- Investment in network industries is not substantial.
- Vulnerability to fluctuations in commodity prices and dependence on Chinese imports.
- Electric and road infrastructure is insufficient for the size of the territory.
- Lack of qualified workforce. The activity rate of the working population is rather low, in particular among women and young people.
- Persisting economic inequalities resulting in political and social tensions (e.g. strike in mining sector).
- Small, open economy vulnerable to external shocks given the dependence on copper and Chinese demand.
- Exposure to climate and earthquake risks.
- Weak budgetary resources: 20% of GDP.
- Inadequate research and innovation.
- Vulnerability of the road network and electricity grid; high energy price/stretched country.
- Income disparity and poor education system.

Chile's foreign investment policy is conducive to foreign investment. The policy is based on simplicity, transparency, and nondiscrimination toward foreign investors. Over the past years, the Government has worked to simplify investment procedures. Foreign investors benefit from a moderate corporate tax and are guaranteed access to the formal foreign exchange market. Foreign investors are allowed to freely remit capital and profits. Chile offers investors a range of solutions and has established a package called "The Innovation Policy Platform" to encourage investment. These

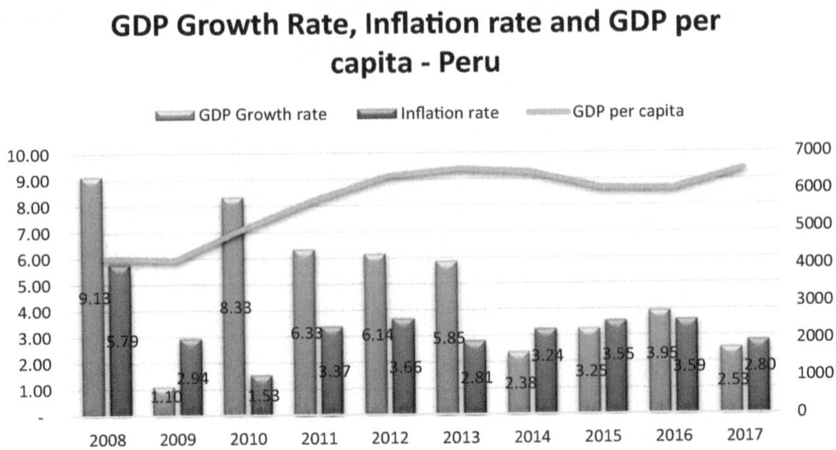

Fig. 6.17 Macroeconomic indicators of Peru (*Source* World Bank data 2019)

measures have notably led to the development of a new type of company that allows a foreigner to create a business in Chile without needing a local partner. Also, joint stock companies can be formed without a local partner. All these policies led to an increase in FDI for Chile.

In 2016, the Government established a new foreign investment promotion and attraction strategy that included the creation of a new national investment promotion agency called "InvestChile". InvestChile assists overseas companies with their investments in Chile. The Government has identified five priority sectors for investment: mining industry services, sophisticated food industry, exportable technological services, tourism, and energy/logistics.

6.7.2 Peru

Peru's economy managed to exhibit progress despite weathering some trouble. Here are some of the strength of Peru's economy.

- Economic dynamism with a sustained growth rate for five years: 2.5% in 2017 (Fig. 6.17) and forecasts up to 3.8% in 2018.

- An abundance of natural resources (mining, energy, agriculture, and fisheries), generating a general trade balance surplus thanks to its numerous exports.
- Sensible macroeconomic policies that have been carried out by an independent central bank, which has enabled the country to have optimal management of the public debt and to reduce the external debt.
- A large workforce because of the youth of the population.
- Favorable development of the domestic market, encouraged by ever stronger domestic demand.
- Membership in the Pacific Alliance, which opens access to the markets of Chile, Colombia, and Mexico.
- Low level of public debt.
- Tourist destination.

Despite having tremendous potential, Peru has always failed to live up to the hype. Peru needs to address how it can overcome the following weakness in its economy.

- High vulnerability to commodity prices and the Chinese economy.
- High dependence on exports in the primary sector.
- Legal framework with deficiencies that do not help eradicating corruption.
- A social situation that is sometimes difficult depending on the region, caused by a structuring of the redistribution of unstable and unequal wealth.
- A large lack of infrastructure.
- Vulnerability to natural disasters.
- A large informal sector (70% of employment in 2017 according to COFACE).

Peru started promoting liberalization policies since 90s along with stabilizing the economy. Peru dropped customs barrier and opened its economy to foreign investors. Continuing with that philosophy, in 2002 Peruvian government established an agency called "Pro-inversion," which was aimed to promote and administer private investment in Peru. "Pro-inversion" successfully participated in privatization of public companies and industries based on natural resources (IMF economic success report on Peru, 2015).

IMF and World Bank supported the legislative reforms and privatizations by disbursing a loan amount close to US$7 billion between 1990s and 2010. Peru continues to impress the world with its strong economic showing and has a great future ahead.

6.8 Conclusion

6.8.1 Chile

Chile had an average annual growth rate of only 1.7% through the 2014/2017 period. In 2018, GDP observed a sharp improvement. The stronger performance was primarily because of relatively higher copper prices and the rebound in business confidence. These factors also contributed to a rebound in investments after four consecutive years of retrenchment. A low inflation level and an appropriate monetary policy have contributed to improving household consumption. In 2019, investments should remain robust. Household consumption might deceleration due to the side effects of inflation moving back to the 3% target, and the central bank implementing a tightening monetary cycle.

Employment data, however, is less than satisfactory due to growing labor force. Potential future risk comes from a rise of the US–China trade war, that could hurt global growth and copper prices. China and the United States are the primary destinations of Chile's exports, accounting for 28 and 14% respectively of total exports in 2017. As Chile is the lead copper producing country of the world, copper accounts for 10% of the country's GDP, 25% of its fiscal revenues, and 50% of its export earnings.

The current account deficit broadened in 2018. This is mainly due to the trade balance. Higher energy price drove imports while weaker copper price slowed down exports. Copper and energy prices are expected to remain at the same levels in 2019, so no big changes in balance are expected. Foreign direct investments are enough to compensate for deficit balance. Chile holds foreign exchange reserves worth roughly 14% of GDP, or seven months of import coverage, in addition to sovereign wealth funds estimated at around 9% of GDP. Chile has an external debt of 60% of its GDP, over 70% of which is owned by the private sector. 21% of is owned by banks and financial institutions, 79% by nonfinancial institutions. In 2019, fiscal consolidation is expected to gain further momentum and bring prosperity to Chile.

6.8.2 Peru

2017 was a turbulent year for Peru. First, it was a massive flood then it was suspension of infrastructure project and public investment due to corruption scandal. Nevertheless, Peru's GDP saw marked improvement in 2018. In this period, domestic demand has increased significantly and investments made a comeback. A strong political environment favored investment from both private and public sector. In 2018, household consumption also increased because of prudent monetary policy that resulted in measured inflation.

2019 should be a good year for Peru. There shouldn't be much change in import and export. Household consumption is expected to remain steady. Monetary policy is expected to have controlled inflation. Potential future risk comes from a rise of the US–China trade war, that could hurt global growth and copper prices. China and the United States are the primary destinations of Chile's exports. A stronger tightening in US monetary policy can also affect Peru in adverse way.

In the last two years, Peru has accounted for low deficits in its current account, driven by stronger trade surpluses due to improvements in terms of trade. In addition, the low external imbalance has been comfortably covered by high FDI. Peru's international foreign exchange reserves are among the highest in the region relative to GDP, at 29.5% as of the end of 2017.

Peru also has low public debt, due to its wise fiscal policy. All measurable point to a bright future for Peru in the coming years.

References

Alvarado, Rafael, María I. ñiguez, and Pablo Ponce. 2017. Foreign Direct Investment and Economic Growth in Latin America. *Economic Analysis and Policy* 56 (December): 176–187.

Amidu, Mohammed. 2006. The link Between Monetary Policy and Banks' Lending Behavior: The Ghanaian Case. *Banks and Bank Systems* 1 (4): 38–48.

Calvo, G., L. Leiderman, and C. Reinhart. 1993. Capital Inflows and Real Exchange Rate Appreciation in Latin America. *IMF Staff Papers* 40: 108–151.

Celis, C., and G. Maturana. 1998. Initial Public Offerings in Chile. *Abante* 1: 7–31.

Corbo, Vittorio, and José Miguel Sánchez. 1985. Adjustments by Industrial Firms in Chile During 1974–82. In *Scrambling for Survivaled*, ed. V. Corbo and J.de Melo. Staff Working Paper No. 764, World Bank, Washington.

De la Rocha, Javier. 1998. The Transmission Mechanism of Monetary Policy in Peru' in the Transmission of Monetary Policy in Emerging Market Economies. Bank for International Settlements Policy Papers, No. 3.

Edwards, Sebastian. 1984. The Order of Liberalization of the External Sector in Developing Countries. Princeton Essays in International Finance No. 156. (December).

Harberger, Arnold. 1985. Observations on the Chilean Economy, 1973–1983. *Economic Development and Cultural Change* 33 (April): 451–462.

Haslam, P.A., and N.A. Tanimoune. 2016. The Determinants of Social Conflict in the Latin American Mining Sector: New Evidence with Quantitative Data. *World Development* 78: 401–419.

http://data.imf.org/. Accessed multiple times latest May 12, 2019.

https://data.oecd.org/chile.htm. Accessed April 11, 2019.

https://data.worldbank.org. Accessed multiple times latest May 12, 2019.

https://en.portal.santandertrade.com/establish-overseas/chile/foreign-investment. Accessed May 11, 2019.

https://en.portal.santandertrade.com/establish-overseas/peru/investing. Accessed March 14, 2019.

https://tradingeconomics.com/chile/rating. Accessed April 13, 2019.

https://tradingeconomics.com/peru/stock-market. Accessed May 2, 2019.

https://ustr.gov/trade-agreements/free-trade-agreements/peru-tpa. Accessed February 11, 2019.

https://www.coface.com/Economic-Studies-and-Country-Risks/Chile. Accessed May 11, 2019.

https://www.coface.com/Economic-Studies-and-Country-Risks/Peru. Accessed May 11, 2019.

https://www.export.gov. Accessed April 2, 2019.

https://www.forbes.com/sites/jonathanmoed/2018/11/19/start-up-chiles-impact-2010-2018-inside-the-revolutionary-startup-accelerator/. Accessed January 4, 2019.

https://www.forbes.com/lists/2011/6/best-countries-11_Chile_CHI020.html. Accessed March 16, 2019.

http://www.sseinitiative.org. Accesses May 2, 2019; Accessed April 11, 2019.

http://www.svs.cl. Accessed May 2, 2019.

https://www.worldatlas.com/articles/the-world-s-leading-silver-producing-countries.html. Accessed March 14, 2019.

https://www.worldatlas.com/articles/the-richest-countries-in-south-america.html. Accessed April 12, 2019.

Liberalisation, Crisis, Intervention: The Chilean Financial System, 1975–1985. In *Banking Crises: Cases and Issues*, ed. V. Sundararajan and T. BaliÒo. Washington, DC: IMF.

Luders, Rolf. 1986. Lessons from the Financial Liberalization of Chile: 1974–1982 (Unpublished). Washington: World Bank. (June).

Mayer, Enrique. 2009. *Ugly Stories of the Peruvian Agrarian Reform*. Durham, NC: Duke University Press.

McKinnon, Ronald. 1973. *Money and Capital in Economic Development*. Washington: The Brookings Institution.

McKinnon, Ronald. 1982. The Order of Economic Liberalization: Lessons from Chile and Argentina. In *Economic Policy in a World of Change Carnegie-Rochester Conference Series on Public Policy*, vol. 17, ed. Karl Brunner and Allan Meltzer.

Opazo et al. 2014. Institutional Investors and Long-Term Investment Evidence from Chile. World Bank Working Paper. Development Research Group Macroeconomics and Growth Team June 2014.

Posner, P. 2008. *Canadian Journal of Latin American and Caribbean Studies/Revue Canadienne Des études Latino-Américaines et Caraïbes* 33 (65): 223–225.

Scully, Timothy R. 1992. *Rethinking the Center: Party Politics in Nineteenth- and Twentieth-Century Chile*. Stanford: Stanford University Press.

U.S. Geological Survey, Mineral Commodity Summaries, February 2019.

CHAPTER 7

Establishing Business in Chile and Peru

7.1 Introduction

Being able to establish a business in Chile or Peru is an opportunity waiting to happen. Both countries have demonstrated over the most recent decades their ability to grow, innovate and reach levels of economic development that were not thought of in the latter part of the twentieth century. Both countries are sustaining their growth and development. Peru has had some political turbulence with its President Pablo Kuczynski having to resign because of his involvement in financial scandal. His successor, President Martin Vizcarra appears to have gained control of the country and is on a positive trajectory toward goal attainment. For businesses who are interested in international foreign investment seeking out opportunities in Peru or Chile has a variety of prospects. While there are opportunities there are some major challenges that every investor has to consider before a decision is made to invest in property, products or services in Chile or Peru. Later in this chapter, we will talk about some of the major issues that investors will face as they make decision about investing in these countries.

7.2 Background

There are two major areas of interest for almost every business investor, (a) what is the length of time it takes to start up a business in a country, and (b) in what condition is the country's infrastructure. Both of these

J. E. Spillan and M. N. Rahman, *Doing Business in Chile and Peru*,
https://doi.org/10.1007/978-3-030-25073-7_7

questions have major impact on a positive or negative decision to invest or not to invest.

The first question about what is the length of time it takes to start up a business is important because if it takes a great deal of time, a business person can lose business opportunities. It is necessary for the businessperson to find out all he/she can about the tasks and procedures necessary to legally form and operate a business. Having this information will give the business investor knowledge to develop a strategy or strategies in order to meet the business start-up requirements. So, it is important that the investor gather as much information as possible to be informed as to what is included in this dynamic process. Since time is money and the opportunities pass rapidly the investor has to work thoroughly and quickly. Later in this chapter we will outline many of the steps and procedures that are needed to start-up a business in the respective countries.

Another of the major issues that every business person asks when thinking about investing in an international environment is: What condition is the country's infrastructure? This is a critical question because if the manager cannot efficiently and effectively move goods from one point to another, then the business costs become prohibited and the investment is not worth the time and energy in operating the business. Even outsourcing the logistics can be problematic and costly if the infrastructure is weak, unstable and not able to move goods efficiently. We will also spend considerable time discussing this topic in later sections of this chapter.

7.3 Investment in New Venture Business—Financial Issues, Financial Markets

7.3.1 Franchising

Four hundred and seventy-five companies in Peru are involved in franchising. The companies are involved mainly in the food service sector. Of the 475 companies, 85 are United States and 239 are Peruvian. The concept of franchising as a means of establishing a business has seen rapid growth in Peru. It is presently growing at a rate of about 20% per year. The primary location of franchises is in shopping centers. Since lots of consumers visit shopping centers, this has attracted many of the franchising activities. Peru has 85 shopping centers of which 45 exist in Lima and 40 are found outside of Lima.

Franchising has amounted to more than $7 billion dollars in the Peruvian economy (www.export.gov, Franchising, 2018).

In another form of market entry in which the franchisor provides the franchisee with intangible property and other assistance for a prolonged period of time. Franchising gives company more control over sale of products in the target market. Management contracts and turn key projects are also important methods of market entry. The management contract's advantage is that it saves time and resources, provides expertise and business continuity. For the turnkey projects it requires less management work, reduces timelines, and cost overruns (Wild and Wild 2019).

Peru initiated an implemented new policy to start a business. The new rules reduce the time to procure municipal licenses and building inspection. When compared to other Latin American countries Peru has 245 days or 10 days per capita to start a business while the average in Latin America and Caribbean is 28.5 and 38% per capita income.

Peru further has improved the quality control of construction. By increasing the qualifications requirements of professionals who do inspections, Peru has provided a higher standard with less hassles. The reinforcement of high standards in construction protects the public and makes doing business much safer.

Peru is the top performer in Latin America with regard to registering property. In Peru, it takes 7.5 days to transfer property title while in the Latin American region it generally takes 63 days (Peru 2017).

Peru is one of the most stable economies in the Latin American region. It is the 6th largest economy in Latin America and 7th among the top 20 border countries like Russia, Mexico, and South Africa (Santarini 2017).

7.3.2 *Market Challenge in Peru*

Some of the outstanding issues that have come to light among business investors are as follows:

a. Inefficient government procurement procedures
b. Reluctance of some government people to make final contracts for fear of liabilities
c. Some business people find it difficult to resolve disputes with government
d. Some have reported difficulties securing legal solutions to commercial disputes (www.export.gov, Marketing, 2019).

7.4 Distribution and Focus—Supply Chain Management Issue

Global Supply Chain is a critical part of doing business internationally. Just about all businesses depend on a dependable supply chain to successfully operate their business. Offering products and services cheaper, and to more customers in a broader range of marketplaces requires well-functioning supply chains.

The logistics part of supply chain management requires suppliers to provide timely delivery of goods to the appropriate destination. Managing the physical flow of goods from point of origin as raw materials to end users as finished products is a significant process that has to be managed correctly. Completing this function internationally can be difficult due to the cross-border transfers of goods. Improper management of logistics can become very costly for businesses. Cost of transporting materials and finished goods affects many decisions about where to locate manufacturing and distribution facilities. Depending on the location of these facilities the cost of movement of goods can be very cheap or very expensive. Supply chain and logistics decisions are critically important to any business (Wild and Wild 2019).

Distribution channels are intermediary specialist firms that provide various logistics as part of an international supply chain process. This function requires the movement of goods to their destination be it a market or other member of the supply chain. Independent distributors provide distribution and marketing services to local firms in contracted areas (Cavusgil et al. 2017).

7.5 Agencies and Licensing

Licensing

Licensing is a relationship between an owner of generally intellectual property or the licensor and the user, the licensee. For instance, high tech companies regularly license their patents and knowhow to foreign companies. Copyrights and trademarks come into this category of regulation and control. Many times, it becomes a mechanism for entering a country or industry (Cavusgil et al. 2017).

7.5.1 Peru—Licensing

Licensing
International businesses enter licensing agreements to provide a company with access to special technology, equipment or locations. It is an easy mode of entry into a country and a market that can be full of potential. Obviously, the licensor and licensee have to agree on a price and the terms of the license agreement. This method of market entry has some advantages. These advantages are listed below:

a. Can be used to finance international expansion
b. It is a less risky approach to international expansion. It shields the licensor from increased risk of operating own production facilities
c. Decreases the opportunity that licenses good/products will be introduced to other close markets.

Licensee can use it as a vehicle for upgrading its production technologies.

Peruvian law allows for joint venture agreements with local partners. This is popular in the textile industry (www.export.gov, Licensing, 2018).

7.6 Physical Infrastructure and Supply Chain Management

A major indicator of economic development is the extent and breadth of a country's infrastructure. These include paved roads, railroads, seaports, communication networks, financial networks, energy supplies, and distribution networks. These elements support the production and marketing functions of businesses. The quality of the infrastructure is also a major issue because it affects the ability to transact business operations and effectively engage in business development. Without appropriate transportation facilities, distribution costs can increase substantially and the ability to reach relevant are weakened (Cateora et al. 2016).

The existence of a well-developed and efficiently operated infrastructure is crucial to any effective supply chain anywhere in the world. A good infrastructure in a host country affects the decision to locate a business in that country. Well-developed infrastructure can significantly decrease the distance between regions and can integrate markets and connect other markets throughout the country (Srinivasan et al. 2014).

Well-developed modes of transportation such as roads, railroads, ports, and air transport allow businesses to move goods and services to and from markets in a timely and secure fashion. Having an effectively developed electrical system that can supply businesses with consistent, reliable and timely flow of electricity is of critical importance to any business formation and sustainable enterprise. A telecommunication system that provides a network for swift and effortless flow of information is imperative. To successfully operate a business, all of these infrastructure elements are needed (Srinivasan et al. 2014).

7.6.1 *Logistic Assessments*

The capacity of developing countries to efficiently move goods and connect manufacturers and consumers with international markets is improving—albeit slowly. But much more is needed to close the existing "performance gap" between high and low performers. Supply chains are only as good as their weakest link, and sustainable improvements require complex changes in a range of policy dimensions in areas including infrastructure, trade facilitation, and services. These efforts require focus and persistence—a combination few countries have achieved so far, according to a new World Bank Group survey on trade logistics (World Bank 2018).

* * *

The LPI or logistics performance index is a bench mark tool that gives information for gauging the challenges and opportunities that countries encounter in performance of their trade logistics.

The following tables outline the rankings of both Chile and Peru according to the World Bank assessment methods.

Table 7.1 provides an assessment benchmarking tool created by the World Bank to help countries identify the challenges and opportunities they face in their performance on trade logistics and what they can do to improve their performance. The LPI index is low at a score of 1 and high at a score of 5. As such we see that Chile is doing very well while Peru is more than half of the high score.

The foregoing Table 7.2 shows the relative metrics for movement of goods according to the main logistics areas. This data provides a good understanding of how effective and efficient the logistical operations among supply chain operators is in Chile and Peru.

Table 7.1 Logistics performance index (LPI): Assessment

Country	*Year*	*LPT rank*	*LPT score*	*Customs*	*Infrastructure*	*Global shipments*	*Logistics competence*	*Time line*
Chile	2018	34	3.32	3.27	3.21	3.27	3.13	3.80
Peru	2018	83	2.69	2.53	2.28	2.84	2.42	3.45

Source World Bank—IBRD-IDA, 2018, http://lpi.worldbank.org/international/global

Table 7.2 Domestic LPI performance

Type of item	*Chile*	*Peru*
Export time port or airport supply chain (km)	300	39
Lead time days	3	2
Import times and distances—land supply chain		
Distance (km)	300	84
Days	5	5
Clearance time w/o inspections (days)	5	5
Clearance time with inspections (days)	5	5
Declaration process (days)	1	2
Ability to choose location of final clearance (%)	3	15
Goods released pending clearance (%)	1	4

Source World Bank—IBRD-IDA, 2018, http://lpi.worldbank.org/domestic/performance/2018/CLCHL/

7.7 Negotiation Patterns and Partners

7.7.1 Negotiations

Domestic business negotiations can be challenging. When we add the complications of cross-cultural factors into the mix, it can become a daunting and difficult situation. Culture has a significant impact on business negotiations. Companies and countries do not negotiate—people negotiate (Cateora et al. 2016).

When considering the potential problems in cross-cultural negotiations, especially when there are mixed managers from relationship-oriented cultures such as China or Middle Eastern countries or with those of information-oriented cultures illustrated by the US, Great Britain or Germany—then there is a question of how really negotiations operate successfully with all the pitfalls that are in the negotiators' path. An appreciation of cultural differences can become a very important element of the negotiation process. Four suggestions can modify or reduce some of the complexities in cross-cultural business negotiations:

a. Picking the proper negotiation team
b. Providing proper training, preparation and a good location
c. Negotiation management process or what happens at the negotiating table
d. Pepper follow-up procedures and practices (Cateora et al. 2016).

7.7.2 Chilean Negotiations

Since Chile lies very south in South America, its relationship with many other countries is not as expansive as a country that resides for example in Central Europe where connections to other European countries and societies is very close. The Chilean culture is quite homogeneous. The Chilean culture is group oriented. It requires building relationships and trust. Chileans generally require strong bonds before closing any deals. Chileans want to do business with people they know, like and trust. Because relationships are generally among people rather than companies, building trust is critical to achieving successful business negotiations. Creating business relationships among people and building strong relationships is a typical feature in Chile. Some of the major attributes necessary to be successful in negotiations in Chile are:

a. Character and kindness are essential
b. Communication in Chile is usually direct
c. Sometimes Chileans are reluctant to disagree openly with someone they like
d. It may be good idea to find an intermediary or echufado
e. Senior executives should attend initial negotiation meeting
f. Meeting generally begin with exchange of business cards and small talk
g. Negotiating is a joint problem-solving process in Chile
h. Chileans are generally straight forward negotiators
i. Chileans believe in win-win outcomes
j. Openly aggressive or adversarial techniques are generally avoided
k. Threatening or aggressive action is not acceptable (Katz 2017).

7.7.3 *Peruvian Negotiators*

Peruvian culture is pluralistic (American Indian, Whites and Mestizos) but in many cases has limited exposure to other cultures except its neighbors. As in Chile, the key path to successful negotiations is through the building of lasting and trusting relationships. Nothing is really negotiated until these bonds are established. Some of the features of negotiation in the Peruvian culture and businesses are listed below:

a. People may interact and talk when only about two feet apart
b. Communication is not very direct
c. Peruvian people do not get to the point quickly
d. The directness of communications may be more direct as a relationship grows
e. Body language and gestures can be lively
f. Generally, negotiations in Peru are entered into by individuals or teams
g. Leveraging personal relationships is important in negotiations
h. Primary negotiation style is cooperative
i. Peruvians are a win-win culture (Katz 2007).

7.8 Corporate Social Responsibilities (CSR)—Sweatshops, Bribery, Child Labor

Being a corporate citizen is not just a corporate social responsibility (CSR) program, but it has become a corporate level business strategy. Transparency is becoming a very important aspect of global businesses. This idea is not only in North American businesses but for businesses around the world (Agawal et al. 2018).

Almost all of the multinational mining corporation presently indicate that they follow CSR. Multinational corporations say that they operate sustainable and responsible businesses that protect the environment, respect human rights, and boost human development and advocate for peace. In Peru's altiplano area, the mining companies have not really lived up to their promise to promote CSR when social unrest and confrontation are intense around the mining towns. Such tensions have caused violence to erupt. While companies attempt to evenly distribute the benefits and profits of mining, many times the companies only provide superficial distribution of benefits and thus leave a large number of people denied the rewards they deserve (Gamu and Dauvergne 2018).

7.8.1 *Corruption in Peru*

Corruption continues to be a serious problem in Peru. Many years ago, corruption was the main belief about politicians. Now the people have evidence. This is indicative by the recent resignation of President Pedro Kuczynski for buying votes. Additionally, the Odebrecht scandal and other controversies in 2018 has put all of the living former presidents either in jail or the center of major corruption investigation (Sonneland 2018).

Corruption is a serious problem in Peru. Bribes, irregular payments, favoritism in government bureaucracies plague the business environment in Peru. According to Transparency International Peru scores 105th of 180 nations assessed with a score of 35. Corruption benefits no-one and creates significant dislocations especially in economic development. It destabilizes society and erodes democracy. Corruptions undermines society's institutions causing problems for all people who depend on businesses and government for their own growth and sustainability. The fallout from the Odebrecht construction company scandal has impacted Peru directly. Its former president Pedro Pablo Kuczynski had to resign because of factual information disclosing his taking bribes associated with the Odebrecht construction company (Transparency International 2019).

On April 18, 2019 former President Alan Garcia committed suicide rather than be arrested by the Peruvian police for his involvement with this Odebrecht scandal that is affecting many countries in Latin America.

7.8.2 *CSR in Chile*

There are similarities in the drivers of CSR in developed countries, there are distinct differences as well. Different sectors drive CSR in Chile. When compared to other geographic areas where consumer demand and government regulation provided the impetus for CSR efforts, multinational companies (MNCs) and nongovernmental organizations (NGOs) are key actors in Chile. MNCs imported their CSR beliefs, skills, and processes into Chile. The adeptness in managing relationships with multiple stakeholders and perceptions of authenticity were also critical to the success of CSR in Chile (Beckman et al. 2009).

The Chilean government with President Michelle Bachelet, launched the National Action Plan on Business and Human Rights in August of 2019. This is a detailed plan to monitor, enforce and follow Human Rights abuses in Business and Society and follow-up on resolution of these offenses. Similarly, in Peru, the government began the National Action Plan on Human Rights in 2018 with the object of ensuring that the public and private businesses respect human rights of all people who live in the Chilean society (Chile 2017).

7.8.3 *Corruption in Chile*

Corruption is not a big problem in Chile. There is a low risk of corruption in this country. By and large Chile is the least corrupt country in Latin America. It has strong transparent institutions with effective methods for investigating and reprimanding any company or institution that violates the rules or laws (GAN 2019). Based on 2018 transparency report Chile ranks 27th among 180 countries in the world. This is a good position for the country to be in and is another positive indication that Chile is a great place to establish a business (Transparency International 2019).

7.9 Discussion

Businesses can be established from a couple different ways. One way is to be an entrepreneur and take an idea, start from scratch and develop an operational business. This is not easy because it requires acquisition of resources and the investment of lots of time to a project that may or may not be realized. The other way acquire or invest in an ongoing business; one that has had some years of experience and performance. Another way it to invest internationally where the factors of production (land, labor, capital, and entrepreneurship) are much more reasonable to come by and can be shaped more easily by the investor.

No matter which of the ways an investor chose to establish a business, there are different types of constraints that must be considered in order to get started. In many countries, it could take up to 1 day in New Zealand to 6 days in Chile, to 25 days in Peru, to 97 days in Haiti (World Bank 2019). Because Chile has such a low number of days for getting a business legally established, it has become a very attractive location for business investment. This shortness of time for set up along with a variety of other factors, i.e. infrastructure, financing, and existence of managerial talent all help in making the task of establishing a business and exciting and positive experience. Even with Peru's relatively short time frame (25 days), it is motivating to know that in less than a month a person can have a business up and running. When compared to other global locations Chile and Peru are ideal places to invest not only due to the shortness of time to establish a business but also due to the stability of the politics and economy in each country.

7.10 Conclusion

Business environment attractiveness is a characteristic of both Peru and Chile. They both are prepared and able to deal with ongoing market globalization, internationalization of capital flows and development of new technology and communication mechanisms. The managers and policymakers in each country understand the complexity and temperament of the global market. They also know how competitive world markets have become. The policy makers and managers in these countries also understand the opportunities and challenges that continue to emerge around the world. The constant change in technology along with the massive and rapid movement of information that affect business transactions are factors that have great impact on the business investment process. Even with all of these obstacles and challenges, the business environments in both Chile and Peru are conducive to investment and successful business enterprises. One major and continuing challenge that could derail any substantive investment is corruption. Throughout Latin America, corruption is like a plague affecting almost every country in some way or in some form. With proper policies and establishment of good CSR and ethics businesses and policy makers can minimize the impact of corruption on businesses. The future holds great investment and business opportunities for investors interested in Chile and Peru.

References

Agawal, Dimple, Josh Bersin, and Gaurav Lahiri. 2018. Citizenship and Social Impact: Society Holds the Mirror: 2018 Global Human Capital Trends. https://www2.deloitte.com/insights/us/en/focus/human-capital-trends/2018/corporate-citizenship-social-impact.html?id=us:2ps:3gl:confidence:eng:cons:102218:nonem:na:DbbQosQx:1123237760:339149875829:b:Future_of_Work:Citizenship_Social_Impact_BMM:nb.

Beckman, Terry, Alison Colwell, and Peggy H. Cunningham. 2009. The Emergence of Corporate Social Responsibility in Chile: The Importance of Authenticity and Social Networks. *Journal of Business Ethics* 86: 191–206.

Cavusgil, Tamer, S. Gary Knight, and John R. Riesenberger. 2017. *International Business: New Relities*, 4th ed. New York: Pearson.

Cateora, Philip, R. Mary, C. Gill, John L. Graham, and R. Broce Money. 2016. *International Marketing*, 17th ed. New York: McGraw-Hill Publishing.

Chile. 2017. National Action Plans on Business and Human Rights. https://globalnaps.org/country/chile/.

Gamu, Jonathan Kishen, and Peter Dauvergne. 2018. The Slow Violence of Corporate Social Responsibility: The Case of Mining in Peru. *Third World Quarterly*, published online. http://doi.org/10.1080/01436597.2018.1432349. Accessed April 7, 2019.

GAN. 2019. https://www.business-anti-corruption.com/country-profiles/chile/. Accessed April 19, 2019.

https://www.export.gov/article?id=Peru-Franchising. Accessed March 14, 2019.

https://www.export.gov/article?id=Peru-Market-Challenges. Accessed March 13, 2019.

Katz, Lothar. 2007. *Negotiating International Business*, 2nd ed. Charleston: Booksurge Publishing.

Katz, Lothar. 2017. *Negotiating International Business: Negotiations Reference Guide to 50 Countries Around the World*. Charleston: Booksurge Publishing.

Peru. 2017. National Action Plan on Human Rights 2018–2021. https://globalnaps.org/country/peru/.

Santarini, Maria. 2017. Why Choose to Do Business in Peru? *BizLatin Hub*. http://www.bizlatinhub.com/do-business-peru/. Accessed March 15, 2019.

Sonneland, Holly K. 2018. LatAm in Focus: Why Peru's Political Establishment is Scared. https://www.as-coa.org/articles/latam-focus-why-perus-political-establishment-scared.

Srinivasan, Mandyam M., Theodore P. Stank, Philippe-Pierre Dornier, and Kenneth J. Petersen. 2014. *Global Supply Chains: Evaluating Regions on an EPIC Framework—Economy Politics, Infrastructure, and Competence*. New York: McGraw-Hill.

Transparency International. 2019. https://www.transparency.org/country/PER. Accessed April 19, 2019.

Wild, John J., and Kenneth L. Wild. 2019. *International Business: The Challenges of Globalization*, 9th ed. New York and London: Pearson Publishing.

World Bank. 2019. https://data.worldbank.org/indicator/ic.reg.durs. Accessed April 13, 2019.

World Bank Logistics Performance Index. 2018. https://lpi.worldbank.org/. Accessed April 14, 2019.

CHAPTER 8

Marketing

8.1 Introduction

In the arena of International Business, marketing relates to identifying, measuring, and responding to market opportunities across borders and around the world (Cavusgil et al. 2017).

The marketing environment has a lot of components. Figure 8.1 presents the most dominant factors that affect a businesses' marketing strategies and efforts. When developing the marketing strategy marketers have to think about the impact of how these components interact with each other. The marketing strategy can only work successfully if the interactions of each part or combination of parts successfully complement each other. Constant monitoring of the interaction among the factors and elements of the environment(s) and the marketing components is required to make adjustments or modifications to the marketing strategy.

Figure 8.1 summarizes the component parts and context for establishing, implementing, and maintaining a suitable marketing program for global branding, international pricing, international distribution, and international marketing communication. Effective managing each of these parts is absolutely necessary to have a successful company marketing program and marketing strategy. This framework needs to be sufficiently flexible to adjust to the fluctuations in the external international business environment.

J. E. Spillan and M. N. Rahman, *Doing Business in Chile and Peru*,
https://doi.org/10.1007/978-3-030-25073-7_8

Marketing Strategy

Global Product Branding	International Pricing
International Distribution	International Market Communication

Marketing Strategy

Fig. 8.1 Components of international environment (*Source* Cavusgil et al. 2017)

8.2 Background

Identifying the market segment or target market requires the marketer to divide the customer base into similar groups. This process facilitates in order, the design of a marketing strategy for each segment or target market. These segments generally share similar characteristics across various national markets. The goals are to create unique patterns of consumer needs. With this information the marketer can position the products or services accordingly. Positioning is a marketing technique that motivates the consumer to think about the product/service in a certain way. Adaptation is generally the approach. International marketers have to think creatively and practically in order to make their marketing strategy work (Cavusgil et al. 2017).

Searching out global markets is a constant task of most companies that are interested in expanding and broadening their product or service exposure. This phenomenon is not only affecting large Multinational Corporations or MNCs but also Small Medium size Enterprises or SMEs also. From clothing, auto parts, and food to financial services, consumers are exposed to a vast array of products and services that are from all over the world. Many products even those carrying a US brand, have been manufactured in another country (Grewal and Levy 2017). Even though we hear that globalization is not as popular as it once was, its existence has created great opportunities and market exposure for many growth-oriented businesses. Globalization has reduced cross border barriers, eliminated, in many cases, the time and distance for product/service delivery, standardized laws across borders and globally integrated the production process

(Grewal and Levy 2017). Globalization has created a wide path for marketing to thrive throughout the world.

8.3 Market Research

Before any marketing decision or plan can be thought about, a marketing research study has to be completed. This process involves collecting, recording, analyzing, and interpreting the data in order to assist the marketers in their market strategy decision-making. It is a fundamental and critical task that must be completed if a marketer wants to have any success in marking goods or services in a foreign country. In this marketing research process, businesses need to conduct and analytical process that assesses the geographic and demographic attributes of the target market area where markets can and should be and then drill down on the specific characteristics of that market(s) in order to properly fit their products/services to the market needs and characteristics. Marketing research in an international environment is more complex because there are several variables such as culture, language barriers, geography, political, and socioeconomic factors that are viewed differently than in the usual domestic market. As such, international marketers have to have a broader point of view and must adapt some of their techniques to international environments (Grewal and Levy 2017) (Table 8.1).

To complete this process marketers, need to look at 4 fundamental areas.

The analytical areas need to be fully explored and decisions need to be made regarding the relationship of these areas of interest with the company's product/service marketing strategy.

The economic analysis is one of the most fundamental areas of analysis for evaluating the ability of the market pay for the products/services that a business offers to the consumer. The Purchase Power of Parity (PPP) comes into play and is an important consideration for consumers when purchasing products/services. Using the Big Mac PPP model, Chile and Peru are setting prices below that of the prices in the United States. That is

Table 8.1 Analytical areas for assessing market needs

Economic analysis	Infrastructure and technology
Socioeconomic analysis	Government and regulatory action

Source Adapted from Grewal and Levy (2017)

important because marketers have one of many metrics to use in evaluating the purchasing power of money in Chile and Peru.

Infrastructure and technology are significantly important items in the analysis process. A country's infrastructure—roads, ports, airports, electrical grids, and sewage systems determine the quality of life of the citizens and their ability to obtain products and services. Good roads, ports, and airports are necessary for the supply chains to get goods to the consumer. The electrical grid capability provides Internet power and communication possibilities and supports many other consumer needs. Chile has been successful in developing important transport and water infrastructure (OECD 2017). Peru has been growing rapidly however its infrastructure has significant gaps. Ambitious public–private partnerships have begun to address the infrastructure problems. These projects have offered international investors great opportunities to make solid growing investments in Peru (World Finance 2018).

Government action has an impact on the marketing activities of companies seeking markets in Chile and Peru. Government policies, procedures, and regulations need to be business-friendly. For the most part, this has been an area that both Peru and Chile have been fortunate to have in their respective countries. This is a critical area because if the government constrains business development and marketing efforts then businesses have to make decisions based on the government policies. Having policies and regulations that hinder quick business development then companies will not invest in these countries. Additionally, if the government has levied tariffs and quotas then these will constrain trade and business.

Socioeconomic analysis is necessary to understand how culture affects just about every aspect of consumer buying decisions. The consumer's values, beliefs, and attitudes about particular products, brands, or services, have an impact on the consumer's buying decisions. As such, marketers have to take into consideration product development and product promotion. Consumer lifestyles also is a major consideration among marketers. Lifestyles are determined by culture and lifestyles affect consumer behavior. As such, international marketers must evaluate this variable when making marketing strategy decisions (Grewal and Levy 2017).

The other major marketing issue relates to social media and internet marketing. Both of these ideas have a major impact on consumer behavior and consumer buying decisions. Marketers need to consider the popularity of these marketing methods/techniques and understand that they are massively used by the buying public around the world.

Fig. 8.2 Context for a firm's international marketing program (*Source* Adapted from Cavusgil et al. [2017, p. 437])

8.4 Marketing Strategy

So once the market analysis is completed, the marketers need to determine their marketing strategy. The marketing strategy is composed of two major components (a) the target market and (b) the marketing mix that the company will develop to achieve its goals. The marketing mix is composed of the product, the price, the promotion, and the place or distribution of the product or service. Each element of the marketing mix has serious relevance when developing the marketing strategy (see Fig. 8.2—International Marketing Context).

A country's marketing and economic development are closely connected. The economic development stage will tell the marketer what marketing task needs to be developed and implemented. Marketing is constantly adapting and adjusting the challenges of new levels of consumption and consumer needs. Market knowledge is critical to accurately aligning marketing strategy to the economic development levels of a country.

Chile is a country which demonstrates how economic growth can occur with agricultural growth as its economic engine. Agricultural exports have been growing and exhibited star performance over the last decades. Chile is a star player in the global fruit export arena. It has become one of the largest fruit exporters in the world. Technology was applied to grape production, wine production, and salmon production along with a variety of other products. Chile is a major exporter of fish meal (Cateora et al. 2016).

Marketers cannot apply a well-designed marketing strategy in an under-developed country. Marketing efforts must be tailored to each situation and circumstances. Assessing and reassessing the market characteristics is important in order to get the right goods to the right people at the right time. Marketing adapts to the market level of development. As countries develop the distribution the market channel system develops simultaneously. A key element of this is estimating the market potential and devising worthwhile segmentation strategies (Cateora et al. 2016).

8.5 Market Entry Strategy

One major international marketing issue relates to global entry strategy. This could be composed of five major approaches that are generally used by major international businesses. These approaches are as follow:

a. Franchising—contracting between franchisor and franchise, i.e. MacDonald's, Pizza Hut.
b. Strategic Alliance—collaborative relationship with other firm(s), i.e. American Airlines and Air France in the airline industry.
c. Joint Venture, i.e. Sony and PlayStation.
d. Foreign Direct Investment—total ownership of plants and facilities and operations (Grewal and Levy 2017), examples Cormo Ltd., Intra Lighting Ltd.

All of these entry modes have value and relate to the marketing strategy that a company is pursuing. How the company enters a country depends on the strategic marketing goals that the company develops.

Leveraging national identity has become an issue in the global market place. International consumer brand perception of various cultures is becoming important around the world. The national image of a country's products can influence a consumer's buying decision.

8.6 Individual Country Marketing

8.6.1 *Peru—Marketing*

The most prominent selling consideration for products and services in Peru is pricing. Asian products sell more than US and European products. Consumers do, however like US and European products due to quality, durability, and customer support.

The metropolitan areas of Peru's urban areas are target markets for products. However, towns and villages in the Amazon and Altiplano Andean areas do not offer good areas for marketing goods, especially electronic devices. The infrastructure for retail space is not well developed. Much of the geographic area is impoverished. Income levels are very low and living conditions are somewhat primitive relative to that of people living in Lima or other metropolitan areas (www.export.gov, Marketing, 2018).

Most of the transactions in Peru are conducted using:

a. Credit cards
b. Cash
c. Wire transfer

They are also made on a 30-day lag basis where the customer selects the merchandise and then pays 30 days later.

8.6.2 *Direct Marketing in Peru*

This approach to marketing has been around for a long time especially in the service sector. Popular methods such as personal selling, telemarketing, and mailing campaigns are acceptable in Peru (www.export.gov, Direct Marketing, 2018).

8.6.3 *Distribution and Sales*

Thirty percent of all Peru's citizens live in Lima, the capital city. 50% of the GDP is produced around Lima. Their national government is a major buyer of goods and services. Other cities such as Arequipa in the south, and Chiclayo and Trujillo in the North, provide markets and selling opportunities for businesses (www.export.gov, Distribution, 2018). Table 8.2 depicts the household consumption trends over the last decade. One can see the

Table 8.2 Household consumptions over time (Peru)

Date	*Value*	*Change %*
2016	124,798,018,974	1.14
2015	123,385,302,780	−4.56
2014	129,281,188,380	1.81
2013	126,982,909,687	5.90
2012	119,911,900,468	15.55
2011	103,777,640,609	13.95
2010	91,074,908,190	28.15
2009	77,081,971,659	2.37
2008	75,297,282,356	22.47
2007	61,481,221,013	15.30
2006	53,323,233,614	7.94

World Data Atlas (2017), https://knoema.com/atlas/Chile/topics/Economy/National-Accounts-GDP-by-Expenditure-at-current-prices-US-Dollars/Household-consumption

substantial variation but generally steady increase in consumption levels among Peruvian households. Years 2007–2012 are particularly interesting as they produced double-digit increases in consumption even when the world was experiencing an economic recession.

Table 8.2 summarizes the state of household consumption. One can observe that in a 10-year period from 2006 to 2016 there has been a more than doubling of household consumption. This is important data for marketers as they establish their marketing program and marketing strategies.

8.6.4 *Peru—Market Entry*

Having a local representative placed in country to explore market opportunities is important. To set up a network of sales connections and relationships is also an important approach to selling goods and services in Peru. Finally, having a legal expert located in Peru to actually navigate Peru's business establishment policies and practices is a must (www.export.gov, Entry Strategies, 2018).

In Peru, country branding has become more apparent and its national campaign has had an impact on the country's outward image and has been attracting tourists to Peru.

Table 8.3 Household consumptions over time (Chile)

Date	*Value*	*Change %*
2016	158,188,857,064	2.58
2015	154,206,313,424	−6.17
2014	164,347,830,604	−5.77
2013	174,402,618,604	5.90
2012	154,691,143,307	8.59
2011	151,667,766,483	18.99
2010	127,461,519,194	25.79
2009	101,331,241,451	−6.07
2008	197,877,254,451	12.63
2007	95,780,542,302	12.98
2006	84,773,235,851	17.09

World Data Atlas (2017), https://knoema.com/atlas/Chile/topics/Economy/National-Accounts-GDP-by-Expenditure-at-current-prices-US-Dollars/Household-consumption

8.6.5 Chile Marketing

Because of Chile's increasing market size there has been a surge in consumer demand. The improving standards of living have caused many consumers to increase their spending on consumer appliances and other durable items over the last few years. Consumer confidence has clearly improved in 2017 along with raises in wages and an expansion of credit. All of these good business news has sustained consumer consumption. Price is an important factor, but quality, service, technology, and durability of the products have become major issues among Chilean consumers (Advertising and Marketing in Chile 2019).

Since their disposable income is rising, Chileans have been able to purchase not only necessities but also electronic goods, phones, and computers, among other desirable products. Increasing purchasing power because of good economic policies has allowed Chileans to purchase better health care and education (Advertising and Marketing in Chile 2019). Table 8.3 depicts the household consumption trends over the last decade. One can see the substantial variation but generally steady increase in consumption levels among Chilean households. Except for 2009, the years 2007, 2008, 2010, 2011 all presented double-digit increases in household consumption in Chile. The year 2009 can be explained by the worldwide economic recession.

Table 8.3 summarizes the state of household consumption. One can observe that in a 10-year period from 2006 to 2016 there has been a less than doubling of household consumption. This is important data for marketers as they establish their marketing program and marketing strategies.

8.6.6 *Future Markets*

Demographics are playing a major role in the future of Chilean markets. The new middle class has been directing their attention on consumption now that they have the disposable income to spend on products and services they desire. Older adults are also a growing market that needs to be addressed. Women between the age of 30–50 years old have desires for products and services. Finally, the millennials. They want clothes, personal care items and other consumer items and services that will satisfy their needs (Advertising and Marketing in Chile 2019).

8.6.7 *Automobile Parts*

With the automobile sector growing, there has been an increased demand for auto parts. Chile has 5.5 million vehicles on the road. In 2018, car sales in Chile was the fastest growing consumer goods category in all of Latin America. New car sales increased by 19.1% in 2017 with truck sales very strong at 94%. The good auto sales market benefits the auto parts businesses. While local manufacturing relates to tires, filters, screws, and gearboxes, most of the accessories (90% of them) are imported. Areas to invest in are engine kits, differential gears and clutches, ring accessories, batteries, and oil, among others (www.export.gov, Chile, Automotive Parts, 2018).

8.6.8 *Market Challenges*

Several aspects of the Chilean market can be a challenge for investors. These challenges are listed below:

a. High degree of competition
b. Relatively small markets
c. Chilean business people are very conservative and cautious
d. Patience and tolerance are needed while waiting for permits and approvals

e. Less than 5% of the people speak English (export.gov, Chile, Market Challenges, 2018).

8.6.9 Chile Market Entry Strategy

By and large recommendations for entering the Chilean market indicates that establishing a local subsidiary or branch office in Chile is the best way of doing business. Furthermore, appointing an agent who has access to buyers and technological expertise can go a long way in establishing a presence or investment and sales capability in Chile (export.gov, Chile-Market Entry Strategy, 2018).

8.6.10 Chile and Agricultural Equipment

One of the most active and central businesses actively operating in Chile is Agriculture. It represents 28% of the total Chilean trade and 11% of its GDP. Chile's economy is propelled by exports such as forestry products, and fishery products. This sector of the economy has approximately 4% growth in 2018.

The major challenges facing the agricultural sector are as follow:

a. High labor costs
b. High energy costs
c. Water resources have been scarce recently

The US, Italy, and Germany are the main suppliers of agricultural machinery and equipment for Chile. China is not far behind with a major interest and investment in doing agricultural equipment business with Chile (export.gov, Chile, Agricultural Equipment, 2018).

Chile has indicated that it is focusing on technology as a means of addressing the lack of labor and water resources needed for production.

8.7 Discussion

Business investors can make a choice in both Chile or Peru and have success. Both countries have become powerhouses in import and export activities. Their business development framework and the consumer population have evolved enough to be capable of sustaining a vibrant consumer-based consumption environment. As the population grows, as citizens' income increase, more markets will develop, and more consumer needs will require satisfying. Marketing in Chile or Peru offers a variety of different alternative. There are the consumer platforms i.e. the retail environment this is growing rapidly. There is also the import and export marketing opportunities because both countries have ambitions industries that furnish finished products to sell internally and around the world. There is the manufacturing arena where Chile furnishes opportunities in wood, cement, copper, and fish processing. Peru also has some major areas of manufacturing such as pharmaceuticals, machinery, fish meal, and textiles.

The Chinese company named Didi Chuxing, a transportation company that connects users of its smartphone apps with vehicles and taxis for hire, has already found opportunities in both Chile and Peru and is launching their business in both countries. Because Chile and Peru have fast growing markets, Didi believes that these two countries have shown such great promise expanding to these Latin American countries is important and a great marketing opportunity.

For those investors who are interested in any of these industry opportunities both Chile and Peru offer great prospects financially. Researching and studying the business and industry environments of these two powerhouses will give the investor an objective perspective of where to invest and how their marketing goals can be achieved by using the resources and talents of Chile and Peru.

8.8 Conclusion

Marketing is at the heart of business success. If firms cannot market their products and services successfully then they cannot sustain their business. In the contemporary world, marketers have to constantly respond to the unending and rapid change in the business environment. The digital age has produced an endless flow of important marketing information that impacts almost all business decisions. The existence of this heavy flow of information presents both opportunities and threats. Therefore, business investors must realize that all business strategy is marketing strategy. The ability to select marketing strategies that fit the country's business environment is an important skill set. Equally important is the ability to continually change and upgrade marketing strategies as information about the environment changes.

Chile and Peru offer business investors lots of marketing possibilities. As they would in any prospective business environment, marketers need to do their homework before they venture into unknown territory. While Chile and Peru offer great positive business options, marketers need to complete the proper marketing research to understand the business ecosystem that exists in these countries. Both countries have constantly changing business environments that have to be monitored. With the technology and business skills that exist today, knowing what the risks and possibilities are is an imperative. No doubt as the Chilean and Peruvian markets change so with the need to evaluate and modify marketing strategies. This is a given in the rapidly changing global business environment.

8.8.1 Business Examples

The following presents some successful businesses that have been established in Peru and Chile over the years which have demonstrated success to its owners, employees, community, and country:

A good example of a small but successful **Peruvian** company.

8.8.2 Peru

In 1988 young Peruvian businessmen decided to establish a hamburger business in Peru. At that time hamburger restaurants were not very popular in this area of the world. With lots of enthusiasm, energy, and drive, they successfully established a hamburger restaurant.

None of these young businessmen had any experience in the restaurant business nor in the area of making or selling hamburgers or other foodstuffs. Using a special and unique recipe, they were able to create a burger that was attractive to the Peruvian population. They implemented innovative ways to present their products, created an environment that people liked to visit and became very efficient in their business practices. With a great product, a colorful venue and excellent service, Bembos became a leader in the field and very competitive with the main chain restaurants that were emerging around the country. Presently they have business locations in Lima, Trujillo, Chiclayo, Piura, and Cuzco. This example shows how a business can grow from nothing to a great and successful business operation in Peru (Bembo 2019, https://www.bembos.com.pe/).

8.8.3 *Chile*

Another example is CCU (Compania Cervecerias Unidas, SA.N) which was founded in 1902. This company produces both alcoholic and non-alcoholic beverages, also operating in the food sector. They have operations in Chile, Argentina, Bolivia, Colombia, Paraguay, Uruguay, and Peru. CCU is Chile's biggest brewer, the second largest soft drink producer, the second largest wine producer, the largest bottler of mineral water, and nectar in Chile. Additionally, CCU is the major pisco producers in the region. Besides the beverages, this company also is involved in the manufacture of candy.

The CCU product lines consist of its own brands, as well as licensed and imported brands, maintaining licensing agreements and/or joint ventures a variety of large international brewing companies. Again, another example of a company that has done well and been very successful in Chile and the surrounding regions (CCU 2018, http://www.ccu.cl/).

Both of these business examples are companies that have a tremendous need for expertise in marketing. Every day they have to implement the 4 Ps—Product value, Promotion of the product, correct and competitive pricing, and strategic placement in distribution of the products around their target markets. Being excellent in marketing is critical to the success of these businesses.

References

Advertising and Marketing in Chile. 2019. https://www.nordeatrade.com/no/explore-new-market/chile/marketing. Accessed March 21, 2019.

Bembo. 2019. https://www.bembos.com.pe/.

Cateora, Philip, R. Mary, C. Gill, John L. Graham, and R. Broce Money. 2016. *International Marketing*, 17th ed. New York: McGraw-Hill.

Cavusgil, Tamar, S., Gary Knight, and John R. Riesenberger. 2017. *International Business*, 4th ed. New York: Pearson.

CCU. 2018. http://www.ccu.cl/.

Export.Gov. 2018. https://www.export.gov/article?id=Peru-Agricultural-Sectors; https://www.export.gov/article?id=Peru-Construction-Equipment. Accessed March 14, 2019.

Export Gov. 2018. https://www.export.gov/article?id=Chile-Market-Challenges. Accessed March 14, 2019.

Grewal, Dhruv, and Michael Levy. 2017. *Marketing*, 5th ed. New York: McGraw-Hill.

https://www.export.gov/article?id=Peru-Market-Overview.

https://www.export.gov/article?id=Peru-Selling-Factors-and-Techniques.

https://www.export.gov/article?id=Peru-Direct-Marketing.
https://www.export.gov/article?id=Peru-Distribution-and-Sales-Channels.
https://www.export.gov/article?id=Peru-Market-Entry-Strategy.
OECD. 2017. Introduction to Public Infrastructure in Chile. In *Gaps and Governance standards of Public Infrastructure in Chile*, Chapter 1. Paris: OECD.
World Data Atlas. 2017. https://knoema.com/atlas/Chile/topics/Economy/National-Accounts-GDP-by-Expenditure-at-current-prices-US-Dollars/Household-consumption. Accessed April 13, 2019.
World Finance. 2018. ProInversion Leads Peru's $10.8 bn Infrastructure Development Drive. https://www.worldfinance.com/infrastructure-investment/proinversion-leads-perus-10-8bn-infrastructure-development-drive.

CHAPTER 9

Speculations on Future Trends and Conclusions

9.1 Introduction

Chile and Peru continue to benefit from the sustained growth in globalization. There are so many unexplored economic opportunities out there. But, at the end of the day it boils down to good governance, distribution of wealth and trickles down economy. While both countries pose unique challenges, the future is very bright for potential investors if the cards are properly played.

Chile and Peru share more than just border and pacific coastline. Language, culture, social structure of Chile and Peru are very similar. While a lot of these cultural elements are influenced from developed countries, having a deep knowledge about the unique culture of the two countries can certainly help initiate, develop and continue a successful business relationship there. Chile is classified as a high-income country and Peru is classified as an upper Middle-income country by World Bank. While Chile has been the investor's darling with strong macroeconomic display, Peru did not live up to the potential due to political seesaw, cronyism and corruption. But both Chile and Peru has tremendous upside to grow and would be a very good opportunity for investors to take advantage of the future economic growth of the two countries. Based on World Bank's Ease of doing business ranking Chile ranks 56 out of 190 countries and Peru ranks 68.

J. E. Spillan and M. N. Rahman, *Doing Business in Chile and Peru*,
https://doi.org/10.1007/978-3-030-25073-7_9

9.2 Re-capping

Chile is located south of Peru. Chile also shares border with Bolivia and Argentina. Peru shares border with five countries—Bolivia, Brazil, Chile, Columbia, and Ecuador. Chile has a population of 18 million and Peru has a population of 31 million. For the year of 2017, Chile has a GDP of $277 billion, has a GDP growth rate of 1.49%, per capita GDP of $15,059.53, and per capita GDP (PPP) of $22,767.04. For the year 2017 GDP of Peru is $211 billion, GDP growth rate is 2.5%, per capita GDP is $6172.69, GDP per capita (PPP) is $ 12,236.71. Chile is the leading Silver and Copper producing country of the world and considered the richest Latin American Country. Both Peru and Chile are considered to be the best countries in Latin America for doing business. Both countries displayed how good public policies can shift a country in positive trajectory of prosperity.

Ninety percent of import and export in Peru is done using the vast 6000 kilometer (3728 miles) coastal route Chile has. That is why ports are critical to the business success of Chile. Peru has a strong agriculture sector. Chile has adopted some of the business and economic practice of United States and Europe that resulted in a very good performance. Chile is recognized as a major economic power in Latin America. Peru had some turbulent years with past regimes, but still Peru maintained very strong macroeconomic performance. Peru has more potential to grow and develop in the future based on all the economic indicators.

Both Peru and Chile are ready to adopt ongoing change in market globalization, deregularization, advancement of new technology. The business environment in Chile and Peru are conducive to attracting investors and having successful business enterprise. Corruption, however, works as leakage that hinders the potential. Throughout Latin America corruption is a huge problem. Chile is not affected by corruption as much, but the same can't be said about Peru. Proper policies and transparency will minimize the corruption. The future seems to be very bright for Chile and Peru.

9.3 Implications

The ease of doing business score captures the gap of each economy from the best regulatory performance observed on each of the indicators across all economies in the sample since 2005. An economy's ease of doing business score is reflected on a scale from 0 to 100, where 0 represents the lowest and 100 represents the best performance. The ease of doing business ranking

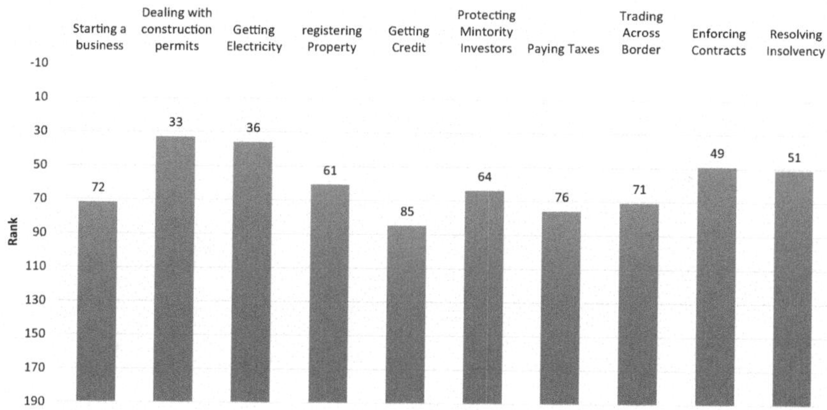

Fig. 9.1 Ranking on doing business in Chile (*Source* World Bank 2019: Doing business report)

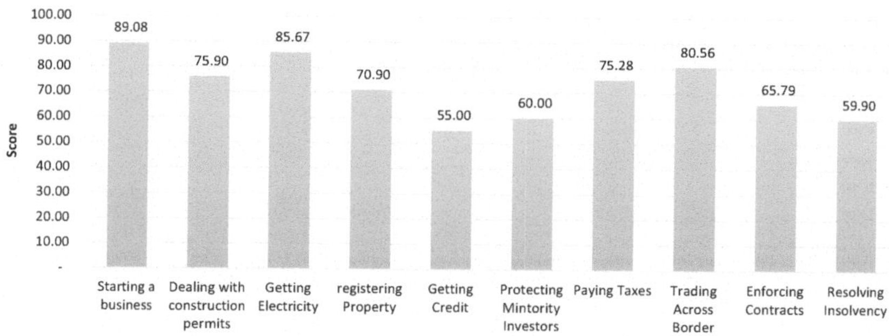

Fig. 9.2 Ease of doing business score in Chile (*Source* World Bank 2019: Doing business report)

ranges from 1 to 190. Chile has a score of 71.81 out of 100 on Ease of doing business report 2019 conducted by World Bank. This score ranks Chile 56 out of 190 countries studied.

Figures 9.1 and 9.2 show Chile ranks very high in dealing with construction permit (33) and getting electricity (36). Chile doesn't rank very high in Getting Credit (85) and Paying Taxes (76). Chile has highest score (89.08) in starting a business and lowest score in Getting Credit (55).

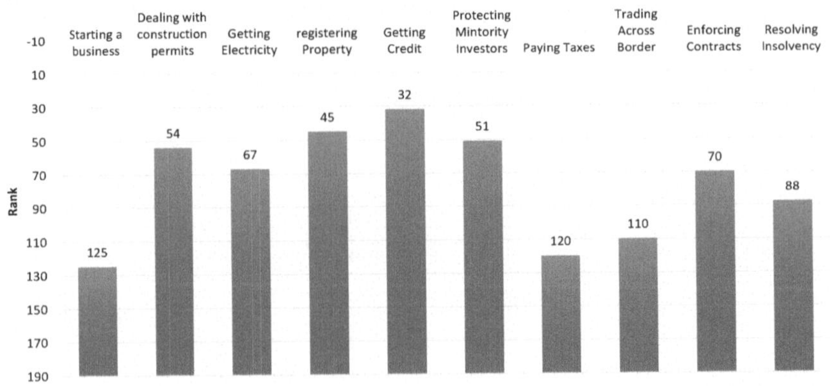

Fig. 9.3 Ranking on doing business in Peru (*Source* World Bank 2019: Doing business report)

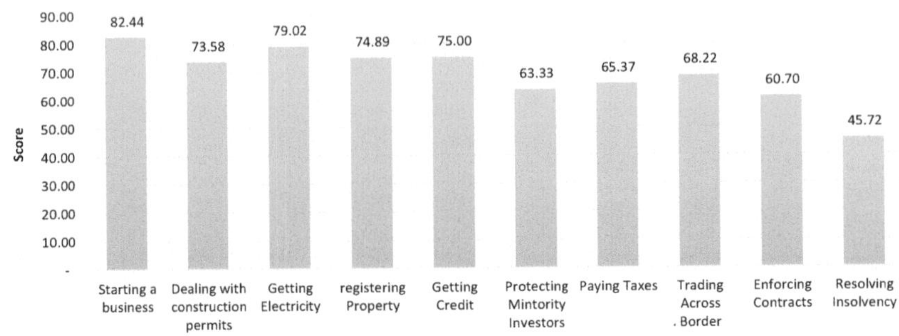

Fig. 9.4 Ease of doing business score in Chile (*Source* World Bank 2019: Doing business report)

Peru has a score of 68.83 out of 100 on Ease of doing business report 2019 conducted by World Bank. This score ranks Chile 68 out of 190 countries studied.

Figures 9.3 and 9.4 show Peru ranks very high in Getting Credit (32) and registering property (45). Peru doesn't rank very high in Starting a business (125) and Paying Taxes (120). Peru has highest score (82.44) in starting a business and lowest score in Recording Inventory (45.72).

9.4 The Challenges Ahead—Next Steps

Although Chile showed progress in recent decades, it still faces significant challenges and opportunities. The fiscal consolidation expected for the medium term will be crucial for stabilizing the debt and consolidating confidence. Government efforts to rationalize the tax system, facilitate employment mobility, reduce bureaucracy, improve the pension system and strengthen the financial system will also be crucial for maintaining growth and reducing Chile's vulnerability to external risks (World Bank 2019).

Growth projections in Peru are vulnerable to external shocks such as a decline in commodity prices or changes in international financial conditions. Events that could trigger these effects include trade protectionism, a deceleration of China's growth or increased uncertainty regarding the financial viability of other emerging economies. The economy is also exposed to natural risks, including recurrent weather phenomena such as El Niño. To address these risks, the Peruvian economy has established monetary, exchange rate and fiscal cushions to mitigate their impact (World Bank 2019).

9.5 Discussion

The economy of Chile has been growing at an impressive rate in the past few decades. The reason behind the growth can be attributed to solid macroeconomic framework. Chile has successfully reduced the population living in poverty from 30% in 2000 to 6.4% in 2017.

Chile had a disappointing GDP growth in 2017, but the economy came back on growth track in 2018, growing at a rate of 4%. This improvement returned more private-sector confidence. Lower interest rates and higher copper prices revitalized mining production. Wholesale trade, commercial services, and manufacturing also progressed during the period.

The current account deficit increased from 2.2% of GDP in 2017 to 3.1% in 2018. It was due to growth in capital goods imports and net foreign assets. This deficit was mainly financed by increased foreign investment, which enabled international reserves to remain stable.

The Peruvian economy has experienced two dissimilar phases of economic development since the turn of the century. Between 2002 and 2013 (except 2009), Peru was one of the fastest-growing countries in Latin America. Peru was maintaining an average GDP growth rate of 6.1% annually. The growth could be attributed to favorable global environment, wise macroeconomic policies, and structural reforms in different areas. These policies created a scenario of high growth and low inflation. The strong growth in employment and income sharply reduced poverty rates. The poverty rate fell from 52.2% in 2005 to 26.1% in 2013. This is equivalent to 6.4 million people escaping poverty during that period. Extreme poverty declined from 30.9% to 11.4% in the same period.

Between 2014 and 2017, GDP growth slowed to an average rate of 3.0%. The primary reason behind that slow growth can be attributed to the decline in international commodity prices, including copper, the leading Peruvian export commodity. This resulted in lower private investment, less fiscal income and weak consumption. Two factors diminished the impact of this external shock on GDP, enabling continued growth, although at a slower pace. The first was the prudent fiscal policy management in terms of monetary and exchange policies. Second was the surge in mining production as projects implemented during the boom years matured, which increased exports and offset the deceleration in domestic demand. In this context, the current account deficit diminished rapidly, from 4.8% of GDP in 2015 to 1.1% in 2017. Net international reserves remained stable at 27% of GDP in August 2018. Average headline inflation was 2.8% in 2017, within the Central Bank's target range.

In 2018, GDP growth has been 2.3% slightly less than the projected growth rate of 4%. This growth was driven by a recovery in domestic demand. Higher commodity prices lead to stronger investment in mining. Rising business confidence, increased loan placement, and increased formal job creation. All of these factors supported private consumption. Public investment has also accelerated in response to increased fiscal spending. A significant increase in tax revenue reduced the fiscal deficit to 2.5% of GDP while the current account deficit increased slightly to 1.5% of GDP. Net international reserves remained stable, totaling 29% of GDP in March 2019. Average inflation stood at 1.3% in 2018, near the lower limit of the Central Bank's target range. At 25.7% (11.4%) of GDP, Peru's gross (net) public debt remains one of the lowest in the region.

9.6 Conclusion

Encouraging innovation, improving the linkage between education and the labor market and promoting the participation of women in the labor market are also essential for improving long-term prospects in Chile and Peru. On the social front, enhancing the quality of health and education services and reducing constraints to access to well-targeted social policies will be key for reducing the remaining poverty and strengthening the middle class. In the medium term, growth is expected to remain close to 4% annually for Peru and slightly lower Chile. This growth rate is projected to be sustained by strong domestic demand and a gradual increase in exports. The fiscal consolidation process will likely reduce public debt by 2021. This economic potential in Chile and Peru is a dream come true for an entrepreneur who is planning to start in a new market.

References

http://data.imf.org/. Accessed multiple times latest on May 12, 2019.

https://data.worldbank.org. Accessed multiple times latest on May 12, 2019.

https://www.coface.com/Economic-Studies-and-Country-Risks/Chile. Accessed May 11, 2019.

https://www.coface.com/Economic-Studies-and-Country-Risks/Peru. Accessed May 11, 2019.

http://www.doingbusiness.org/en/reports/global-reports/doing-business-2019. Accessed May 11, 2019.

https://www.worldbank.org/en/country/chile/overview. Accessed May 1, 2019.

https://www.worldbank.org/en/country/peru/overview. Accessed May 1, 2019.

Index

J. E. Spillan and M. N. Rahman, *Doing Business in Chile and Peru*, https://doi.org/10.1007/978-3-030-25073-7

The manufacturer's authorised representative in the EU is Springer Nature Customer Service Centre GmbH, Europaplatz 3, 69115 Heidelberg, Germany. If you have any concerns regarding our products, please contact ProductSafety@springernature.com

Printed and bound by CPI Group (UK) Ltd, Croydon, CR0 4YY
22/09/2026
02221054-0019